Arthur Mack

Old Man of the Sea

DEDICATION

For Arthur and Gina's children, their families,
and generations to follow

Contents

Illustrations

Acknowledgments

The intent to document Arthur's life was set in motion many years ago by David Houghton, a colleague of Arthur's in the time of the *Invincible* Project and family friend to both Arthur and his wife Gina. Mr Houghton's work, in which he compiled anecdotal information from the first part of Arthur's life, is the foundation of this story.

I called upon two of Arthur's closest friends and work colleagues from days past - John Broomhead and John Bingeman, to continue the project, and without their efforts the book would not exist:

John Broomhead visited Arthur and Gina on numerous occasions for the purpose of conducting interviews, compiling information, and retrieving and digitising family photos that appear in the book. With the contribution of his own personal memoirs, we partnered as co-authors to tell Arthur's amazing story. John's handiwork is also responsible for several images, and the design and production of the book cover.

John Bingeman made significant contributions including anecdotal and factual recollections of his work with Arthur on the *Invincible* and other projects which both men collaborated in over a span of four decades. The 'Bingeman Archive' proved to be a veritable source of documented history respecting Arthur's past accomplishments, not to mention numerous vintage photographs that are featured within.

I was not personally acquainted with Derek Nudd at the start of this project, yet happenstance managed to pair us up with impeccable timing as I sought an editor. As a published author, Derek's skills and expertise proved invaluable in the efforts of editing, typesetting and production of the book.

There are many other people deserving thanks for their contributions, particularly regarding consent for images in the book and other content, namely: the Estate of Robin Gibb, the Estate of Ainsley Adams, Michael Eaton, Dwina Gibb, Keir Hailstone, Dave Rouse, Katy Ball – Collections Registrar with Portsmouth Museum,

Peter Goodwin, Graham Parker, Brian Lavery, Michael J. Allen, Eileen Clegg and Jacquie Shaw with the National Museum of the Royal Navy, Maxine Higgins, Jaime Newell, Melvin Gofton, Joy Terry, Jane Bingeman, and Tony Mack.

And finally – a big thanks to Gina, whom over the course of the project transacted countless email correspondence with me in the effort to collect and affirm book content.

Brent Piniuta

Foreword

Arthur Mack has a lifelong connection to the sea and maritime history. This is a story of his extraordinary discoveries as an amateur archaeologist that have enriched the knowledge of Britain's maritime heritage.

Arthur has managed to document thousands of years of coastal history in Hampshire, and his accomplishments and academic contributions can be found in numerous manuscripts, journals and news articles published worldwide. David R. Houghton, Officer-in-Charge of the Admiralty Exposure Laboratory at Eastney at the time of the first *HMS Invincible* (1744-1758) excavations project, once said *'had Arthur been educated, he would now be a professor in Oxford'*. Arthur is a modest man who self-describes his education as *'being in the mud of Portsmouth Hard'* which is true in both the literal and figurative sense, as his story tells.

This biography and collection of anecdotes from Arthur's life is a tribute to the man, to share his fascinating story as it should rightfully be told. Furthermore, every year it is in publication the proceeds of sale from this book will be donated in Arthur's name to Portsmouth Museum, Historic Dockyard Chatham and Portsmouth Historic Dockyard, for the care and conservation of antiquities and artefacts Arthur has found over the years that now reside in museums, including those from the wreck of eighteenth-century British warship *HMS Invincible* – Arthur's proudest and most indelible find.

Part I

Mudlark

Early Years

Arthur Thomas Mack has lived on Portsea Island, situated on the south coast of England in the County of Hampshire, for his entire life. He was born in College Lane in Portsea – an area of old Portsmouth. Just a few houses down from Arthur's childhood home is St. Georges Square and Britain Street where Isambard Kingdom Brunel, once described as *'one of the most ingenious and prolific figures in engineering history'*[1] was born in 1806.

College Lane is also a stone's throw from Portsmouth Harbour, Victory Gate – formerly called the 'Hard Gate' which is the main entrance to Portsmouth Royal Naval Dockyard, and The Hard, placing his upbringing amidst the backdrop of a gritty port town. 'The Hard' dates from about 1720 and it is believed to get its name from origins as a natural slipway built up for launching and hauling boats in and out of Portsmouth Harbour – it was formed by placing and compacting layers of stone until its surface was packed solid.

The Hard has been a hub of human activity in Portsea for hundreds of years with strong ties to the Dockyard as the area's dominant commercial enterprise and employer of a significant number of local citizens, and of course its national importance as a Naval Base. In the nineteenth century it was known amongst locals as the 'Devil's Acre'[2], having a long-held repute of being frequented by sailors whose ships had been paid off and men coming ashore in search of entertainment, liquor, women, and other pursuits. An editorial from 1859 offered the following narrative:

> *The Hard presents a scene of drunkenness and profligacy which baffles all description.*[3]

Figure 1: *The Common–Hard, Portsmouth* by G. Reinagle, 1834

Arthur's birth on 9th October 1934 placed his beginning in the world during a time of some of the worst economic disparity the United Kingdom has ever seen, the Great Depression, and it is said to have had a pronounced impact on Portsea as it was a poor area of Portsmouth to begin with. Poverty and hardship were rife and had tremendous influence on Arthur as a young child.

To say Arthur had a colourful family and upbringing is most definitely an understatement. Arthur describes his mother Kathleen Mack as having Irish ancestry and in Arthur's youth she was known locally as *'Mad Kit'*. According to Arthur his mother, a housekeeper and homemaker, was of strong character and *'would readily accept a dare to swim across Portsmouth Harbour from Wylie's House to Fort Blockhouse and back in competition with men and boys, and often won'*.

Kathleen had two sisters who sold flowers on the bridge which connects The Hard to the Harbour Railway Station and Gosport Ferry. Arthur relates that one of the sisters, Lottie, *'was unusual in that she smoked a pipe'*. His father, Alfred George Haycock, was *'a hard man'* of Welsh descent who made a living at Flathouse Quay as a stevedore – a longshoreman employed to unload ship's cargo. Despite such demanding physical labour his work did not pay a significant wage and the family lived in destitution.

The family's way of life and circumstances are what Arthur says contributed to him developing *'a quick temper which led me into many a scrape'*. He does not hesitate to share that he grew up in slums and likens Portsea of the day to being like what was characterised in the 1968 film *Oliver!*

At their home in College Lane the children's rooms were on the second floor. Arthur shared a room with his two brothers, and his sister had the second bedroom. The boys' bedroom was approximately 12 x 10 feet in size and had one large bed in which all three boys slept lying *'head to tail'*. With this arrangement their parents slept downstairs in the *'front room with the baby'*. The house had no kitchen to speak of, just a small scullery. In it there was an old butler sink and cold water tap with a small gas cooker alongside it. The only way they could have hot water was to boil a kettle on the old stove. The toilet was outside in the yard adjacent to the rear door. They did not have a bathroom and so they had to use the public baths for washing.

Hunger was an inescapable daily reality, and as young children Arthur and his siblings would stand outside Victory Gate and count on the generosity of the Dockyard workers. Those men, seeing the children often shoeless and in worn clothes, were generous by their nature and would often share their lunches with them. Nourishment was not the only problem Arthur faced, as he recalls their local area of Portsea was rough and lawless; the Police seldom patrolled it and so *'sticking up for yourself'* was essential for survival in their daily lives.

By law children had to attend school, though in reality the boys were expected to undertake some sort of work to support their families with any bit of extra money that could be made. At age seven Arthur joined other Portsea boys to ply the trade of a 'mudlark'. Today, mudlarking is a leisure pastime of scavenging a muddy riverbed – most often associated with the River Thames – in the pursuit of artefacts of daily life from times past, having been cast into or otherwise lost in the water. But at this time in Arthur's life mudlarking was something quite different: the boys worked the mud flats and shallows off The Hard, retrieving coins thrown by entertained travellers walking the bridge to Harbour Station and Gosport Ferry. The boys were in competition to hustle the crowd, daring passers-by with stunts to beckon the toss of a coin that if recovered was theirs to keep.

Figure 2: Mudlarks in Portsmouth Harbour, circa 1930s

Indeed, this activity became a well-known local Portsmouth attraction that provided a reliable income to those who performed. According to Arthur a sixpence (2½p) *'would buy a faceplant into the mud'* and some accompanying antic. A dive into water to recover a coin dropped to the seabed commanded a higher reward. Saturdays during the summer months were particularly profitable for the mudlarks – they entertained captive audiences of holidaymakers standing in queues, waiting for the ferry to take them across the Solent to their getaway retreats on the Isle of Wight.

Competition introduced a hierarchy of opportunity amongst the mudlarks with the highest-profit positions under the bridge being secured by the oldest and largest boys. Each boy kept a tin for the coins he collected. Prospects for theft were ever-present and so each boy had to guard his own tin; fighting amongst themselves was a common occurrence. Loss of the tin or otherwise returning home empty-handed had repercussions, and Arthur recalls a *'backhander'* from Father or a *'clip round the ear'* from Mother. At the end of a 'work day' one would dare not return home covered from head to toe in mud, so Arthur and the others would wash themselves on the shingle bank situated underneath the Railway Station, an area known to the mudlarks as the 'Rammies'.

The boys would not spend their earnings on self-indulgences such as sweets unless a very profitable day allowed an opportunity to skim a bit off the top as their own reward. If lucky, the reward of a penny from Mother for a good day's haul allowed the purchase of a cod's head from the local fish shop for use as bait to catch shore crabs – not for selling but for friendly competition among the mudlarks to see who could take the largest crab. One of the boys' favourite locations for this pastime was Fishermen's Walk, a series of stone block steps leading to the low tide area of the Harbour where fishermen careened their boats. This activity seems to reinforce a camaraderie among the mudlarks; while it was in theory work it was also a way the boys could have childhood fun whilst bonding and developing friendships with one another.

The mudlarks did not go unchallenged. The local Railway Police were forever chasing the boys off the mud and if caught *'a clip round the ear and admonition not to be caught there again'* was the result. According to Arthur a certain delight was had when an Officer lost his shoes, stuck fast in the mud whilst in pursuit of the offenders. When challenged by the school administration for absence or any trouble reported by the police, parents did not officially approve of their children's mudlark activities – but in practice it was an expectation based on the reality of their life circumstance.

For Arthur and the other mudlarks, their childhood and 'careers' came to an end with the Second World War. The Dockyard and Naval Base were highly strategic targets that attracted the attention of the *Oberkommando der Wehrmacht* – the German High Command. Portsea, separated from the target merely by the brick wall around the Dockyard, was vulnerable to attack and suffered during the Portsmouth Blitz, staged by the Luftwaffe which bombed the area relentlessly. More than 60 air raids were staged between 1940 and 1944 and in this time 6,625 houses in Portsea and the surrounding area were destroyed.[4]

Arthur recalls his family home being affected by bombing three times, with the family's possessions including personal items and photos lost in the fray.

Figure 3: Bomb-damaged houses in Hambrook Street, Southsea

After surviving the third air raid Arthur, then age eight, and two of his sisters were evacuated to Totland Bay on the west side of the Isle of Wight. The move did not entirely keep Arthur safe from the perils of war. Counter-invasion measures had been constructed along the coast of the island including anti-tank barricades built of concrete and barbed wire. One day Arthur climbed one of these installations and became entangled in the barbed wire, so badly that he could not free himself. It was by luck that passers-by found him, alerted the local Fire Brigade which attended the scene and cut him free. This must have been a traumatic experience for the young boy and Arthur still has scars on his body from the incident.

The children were billeted with a Mrs Barter, whom Arthur characterised as a stern disciplinarian that you *'were careful not to cross'*. During this time Arthur was enrolled in school, but he confesses to seldom attending as he much preferred being outside searching for fossils that could be found on the island. He also spent time beachcombing and fishing, though fishing was not always to catch fish. American army K-rations, pre-packaged food for troops, often floated into shore for the picking, presumably from a wreck of a US ship that had foundered in the English Channel. The rations were highly coveted as they contained chocolate, coffee, and sugar which at the time were luxuries amid the hardship brought on by the war. It is evident that even with the temporary relocation to Isle of Wight Arthur retained his connection to the sea which from a young age he recognised as having importance and meaning in his life.

After the war's end in 1945 Arthur and his sisters returned to Portsea to find that the family had relocated to Cressy Place in Landport, also not far from the Dockyard. That was not the only surprise, as during the war years Kathleen had four babies. Including Arthur's half-brother, the sibling count would eventually come to be eleven – four girls and seven boys which Arthur retorts was *'a football team'*.

After returning from the Isle of Wight, Arthur was enrolled in a nearby school in Church Street run by the local authority. Because he was eleven years old he stayed there only for about a month, after which he was transferred to the oldest school in the city, opened in 1874, called Portsea Secondary Modern School – formerly The Beneficial School run by charities in Kent Street. Arthur soon reverted to his vices, not the least of which was truancy. In fact, one of his few motivations for going to class was his seasonal side-business of scrumping apples which he in turn took to school and sold them *'six for a penny'*. Aside from that enterprise he returned to his former stomping grounds to re-engage in his mudlark 'career' and fishing. One day whilst catching crabs from the Ferry pontoon he was violently ejected off it into the water after a hard hit from a boat. Two sailors jumped into the water to recover him; he had nearly drowned. With this close brush with death Arthur took to learning to swim from Fishermen's Walk.

The devastation and destruction which resulted from the war also brought new opportunity of finding metal and other materials where bombs had damaged or destroyed buildings in town. Any miscellaneous metal items including shells were collected and traded for money at the scrap merchants, and so this became a new profitable venture. The rubble of many bombed-out Portsea houses was scoured for such bounty. Arthur would venture as far as Horsea Island situated off the northern shore of Portsmouth Harbour to collect anything that could be converted into cash. Scrap lead had other value to Arthur – he needed lead weights for his fishing gear. He once found a small munitions shell which he believed was expended, took it home and put it on a fire to separate what he thought was lead from the rest of the casing. The heat caused it to go off with a spectacular explosion, with shrapnel injuring him in the leg, and for a half hour he could not see. Fortunately, nobody else was injured.

Upon moving to Cressy Place his father had acquired a yard adjacent the Rope Walk, a business owned by a Mr Langford which supplied rope to the Dockyard and other local industry. His father no longer worked as a stevedore and had established a small logging business, and he also repaired and built bicycles as a secondary business to supplement the family income. Arthur was expected to work for him without pay. At this point in his life Arthur was age eleven and an interest in history was stirring within him. He recalls trading one of his father's bicycles for a jadeite green Neolithic axe which was offered up in exchange.

Arthur concedes to a strained relationship between him and his father. He characterises his father as a *'task master'* who drove Arthur and his brothers to work long hours in the yard splitting tree trunks, sawing lumber and cutting wood to be sold for fire-lighting. Arthur felt that this work obligation left him with no life of his own and working with his father so much caused him great frustration. Moreover, his father expected the boys to work at the yard in place of attending school which resulted in the School Inspector making routine visits to the business and even levying fines for disregarding parental responsibility for the children's education. Arthur recalls hiding and occasionally letting the air out of the tyres on the School Inspector's bicycle. Once Arthur was caught in the Yard by the Inspector and led back to class by the ear and received a caning as punishment for his absenteeism. Besides all this drama Arthur recalls shouting, arguments, and even physical altercations with his father. And so at age thirteen Arthur and two friends ran away from home, taking an abandoned boat they had found at Stamshaw and using improvised oars made it as far as Southampton where in town the trio were recognised by the police, apprehended and returned home where discipline awaited them.

Arthur relates a memory from when he was 12 years old, soon after returning from his evacuation to the Isle of Wight:

One day my Father once again kept me off school because he wanted help delivering logs to houses. On the way home after the deliveries, we were sitting on the seat of our horse drawn cart surrounded by loads of dockyard workers on their peddle bikes, riding towards the dockyard gates in readiness to start their day's work. It was a frosty morning and when our horse, named Phil Garlic, made the turn to the right he slipped. He crashed to the ground and the workers on their bikes could not stop in time and slid straight into poor old Phil and carnage ensued. We jumped from the cart and the two of us tried to get Phil up. Unfortunately, he was quite heavy, and his feet kept slipping but we had to keep trying to get him upright once again. The workers were cursing us for stopping them getting to work and all the while Father & I both struggled to get Phil on his feet. Eventually we managed, and all was well. Apart, that is, from the disgruntled dockyard workmen and our wounded pride. I received the normal clip round the ear as if it was my fault – as was normal between Father and Son in our family.

By age fifteen Arthur had enough of family employment and began a job with Plurcrop Midland Cattle Products Limited, an animal waste factory, where he worked a machine that produced sausage casing. It wasn't long after starting this work he had an incident with a faulty cutting guard at his workstation and suffered the loss of a top of a finger, landing him in hospital for six weeks where he received a pedicle graft – the finger end was sutured to his abdomen and when the skin graft growth was complete is was reattached to his hand. Arthur was awarded injury compensation to the amount of £120 – a significant sum of money at the time.

Arthur vividly remembers 14th July 1950 – the day massive explosions rocked the Royal Naval Armament Depot at Bedenham from across the harbour in Gosport. Arthur was bait digging when the first explosion shook the area, the shock of which liquified the mud he was standing in causing him to sink into it. After extricating himself he was headed home on his bike when the second explosion occurred, sending him swerving all over the road. It is said that inadvertent detonation of ordnance aboard an ammunition lighter, which was loaded for transferring munitions to an armament supply-issuing ship, was the cause. The heat of the resulting fire set off 1,000 tonnes of munitions and sent unexploded shells and bombs raining down over a large area. The second blast was set off by the fire, involving an additional 4,000 tonnes of munitions. The blasts and resulting shockwaves carried across the harbour and damaged buildings as far away as Portchester and Fareham. Amazingly there were no fatalities and only 19 people were injured in the incident.[5]

At the age of eighteen Arthur was called up for compulsory National Service and he left Portsea for Wrexham, North Wales for basic training. Upon completion he was drafted to the Pioneer Corps at Wimborne, Dorset. Unfortunately, between his lack of interest in school and the work obligations that supported his family from the age of seven onward, he had left school virtually illiterate. Lacking basic skills in reading, writing and mathematics severely limited any opportunities to receive advanced training and pursue an occupational speciality or technical-based career in the Army. He was assigned to the Catering Corps as an assistant cook, where a significant part of his Army career was devoted to peeling potatoes and learning the basics of cooking. He was chosen for service in the Suez Canal zone and in anticipation of the posting he received the necessary injections. However, the Army's plan changed, and he remained in the UK.

Arthur has no feelings of nostalgia for his time in the Service:

It was a very miserable time for me as I did not like taking orders. I had a very quick temper and spent a lot of time in the guard room. I missed my fishing and being my own boss.

Working Family Man

Happily returning home to Portsea in 1954 after completing his National Service obligations, Arthur had no trouble finding employment. He began work with Wendover's of Southsea, a furniture company, where he made deliveries to customers. He later moved on to Bailey & Whites, a company that imported timber from northern Europe and supplied all the local builders. His place of work was Flathouse Quay where he often put in long nights unloading wood from ships, and while this was hard work the pay was better than his previous earnings. Other duties with the company had him applying fire retardant and rot-proofing chemicals to hardboard. Arthur's brothers Charlie and Patrick also happened to work for the company at the time.

Arthur later went on to take work in the Coppersmith's Shop in Portsmouth Dockyard. Arthur also returned to fishing not only as a hobby but to supplement his income as he had relied upon in the past. He sold his catch, primarily sea bass, to the chef at Keppel's Head Hotel – a posh establishment built in 1779 situated along The Hard, regularly patronised by Naval Officers.

In rare moments of leisure Arthur liked to go skating near the Band Stand on Southsea Common. It was here that one day he met Gina Shepherd of Denmead, a small village on the mainland some seven miles north of Portsea. When they first met, Gina's mother was not at all happy she was entertaining a relationship with him. She recalls that her parents, who lived in a rural setting and were quite conservative, were rather surprised by Gina's choice. Arthur surmises his 'Teddy Boy' attire of the day, *'a long jacket, drainpipe trousers, suede shoes and a bootlace tie'* may not have impressed them.

Figure 4: Gina & Arthur on her 21st birthday and engagement day

On the other hand, all of Arthur's family loved Gina and made her feel welcome every time she visited. Despite what parents thought to be a questionable pairing the couple had little doubt about sharing a life together and were married in Saint Georges Church in Denmead on 21st January 1956.

Figure 5: Gina & Arthur on their wedding day

Their honeymoon was spent fishing for flounder in Port Creek, which may sound unusual to most people but was just right by them. Gina soon learned how Arthur and fishing would become a defining attribute of their lifestyle and livelihood; she recalls a day in their first week of marriage when Arthur brought home a catch of flatfish. Rather than helping clean it he dropped the fish in the kitchen sink and left the task to Gina. She was somewhat perturbed by the experience of the fisheyes looking back at her as she prepared dinner.

Arthur continued working in the Coppersmith's Shop and was earning £7 per week. Weekends found him back on the muddy shores of Portsmouth Harbour using a potato fork to dig ragworm and lugworm which he sold as fishing bait. On Mondays he would visit his primary client Miss Cox of the Salvation Army *'who wanted assurance that the bait had not been dug up on a Sunday'*. He had other regular clients who purchased his bait, and this venture *'was a considerable aid'* to the family's finances.

One of Arthur's other bait customers was Len Bloxham, the proprietor of a small business in Albert Road. In the employ of his shop was a young fellow named John Broomhead who worked there part-time whilst attending school. Bloxham relied on Arthur's bait as a marketable commodity and so he would often send John out to assist Arthur collect bait for resale in the shop. Arthur recalls that John always had the best intentions of helping with the bait digging but he just didn't have the 'knack' required to work in the mud, and often became frustrated with John's 'help'. Arthur remembers at least one occasion when John became completely stuck in the mud and the more he struggled, the deeper he sank. Arthur had to free John by digging all the mud out around him! Little did Arthur know at the time, that decades into the future he would call upon John to help him with what would prove to be an extraordinary find – one that would change the lives of both men forever.

As one might imagine bait-digging resulted in finds other than worms and Arthur regularly came across historical items that captured his interest as much did the Neolithic axe from his childhood. One such find of Arthur's occurred in the 1950s, while working in the northern reaches of Portsmouth Harbour near Portchester Castle. One day the black mud revealed a small statuette of the Japanese rice god *Daikoku*, made of Parian (white marble) ware or Bisque. Arthur had an antique specialist investigate it, to learn its origins dating from the late eighteenth or early nineteenth century. *Daikoku* is a Japanese deity – one of the *Shichi-fuku-jin* or 'seven Gods of luck' – the God of wealth and prosperity. *Daikoku's* association with wealth eventually established a custom in Japanese culture known as the *fukunusubi* or 'theft of fortune'. The custom has origins in the belief that whoever could steal a divine figure of *Daikoku* was assured good fortune – if not caught in the act. Finding the statuette could not have been more telling in predicting, or perhaps even defining, Arthur's life story yet to unfold.

Figure 6: *Daikoku* statuette found by Arthur

Other small finds in the mud of Portsmouth Harbour included numerous clay pipes which sent Arthur to Portsmouth Central Library in a keen interest to date his finds; ultimately the examples he had recovered were from the late sixteenth century up to 1840. Arthur confesses he had difficulty attempting the research due to his lack of education, which came with the realisation that he would need to improve his reading skill to pursue his historical interests.

In 1960 Arthur and Gina relocated to Eastney, the south east area of Portsea Island, and in doing so Arthur left his employment in the

Dockyard. This presented him with new opportunities to dig in his quest for historical items. He took on new employment with Barnes & Elliot Contracting and joined an excavation crew digging the foundations for a new hall at Portsmouth Grammar School. In that endeavour Arthur found an abandoned well that yielded old French and English coins, some of which were sold to a second-hand shop in Marmion Road. The hunt for other vintage coins persuaded Arthur to purchase a metal detector and this acquisition took him to the local beaches between Selsey and Eastney where in the winter months, low water during extreme spring tides often yielded a trove of coins and other artefacts. Arthur recalls that the area behind the Still & West Public House in Old Portsmouth was a bountiful location for beach finds. Scanning areas of the New Forest netted Roman era coins as well. To this day Arthur has many of his early-days finds including two-penny cartwheel George III pieces and an Elizabethan sixpence.

Career Fisherman

In 1967 Arthur decided to leave the security of employment and reliable pay with Barnes & Elliot to make a go on his own at full time fishing – a decision made even more difficult by the fact their third child, Anthony, was born in February. He bought a fourteen-foot open boat with a 4½ horsepower Seagull outboard engine which could tow a ten-foot trawl for catching Dover sole in the waters of the Solent between Eastney and Hayling Island, and south towards the Isle of Wight. While he mainly worked solo, on occasion he would also fish with a friend from time to time. Due to limitations of the equipment he could afford, Arthur had to hand-haul the trawl in and over the sides of the boat, so it was physically demanding work. During summer months Arthur would utilise this method of fishing at night when the catch would be the most productive and he would work extra-long hours whenever the fish happened to be plentiful. He recalls often coming home in the early morning hours *'freezing cold and despondent'*, but this never deterred him as he would always go out the next day or night to earn a living.

He soon reinvested his revenue into a sixteen-foot fibreglass hull from Megan Boatbuilder and fitted it out to his own specification of an inboard 6 horsepower Royal Enfield air-cooled diesel engine; this upgrade allowed a twelve-foot trawl. During the winter months Arthur would go oystering with a hand trawl. Fishing was a physical undertaking and made for long workdays. Managing a trawl would in theory result in a bigger catch of lower value fish, but later in his fishing career Arthur also took to rod and line fishing for sea bass, with better results to his income. This fishing was done during the daytime and Arthur's preferred location was the entrance to Langstone Harbour situated between Eastney and Hayling Island, where a swift tidal run made for an ideal fishing spot. His catch was sold to local fish merchants. Arthur also continued to dig bait when he could, the profits from which made it a worthwhile endeavour.

Figure 7: Arthur fishing in Langstone Harbour in the early 1970s

While Arthur was out on the water working his trade, Gina remained at home taking care of the family. She relates

Sometimes it was inconvenient but in the main it was okay. The two older children were both at school and Tony was just starting school. However, we all found it more difficult when Arthur worked at night. When he had been fishing and for whatever reason came home in the early hours before daybreak, no matter how hard he tried to be quiet he always made a noise, which tended to wake us up.

When the children were all at school, I was able to knit at home for a company called Robin Wools & Emu Wools. They were always getting new patterns to try out and they gave the trials to me – this was very convenient

to be able to work from home. At Christmas times, the Post Office always
wanted part time staff to work in the sorting office and I managed to work
for them every Christmas for 10 years. This was a handy addition to our
income because generally speaking, Arthur would be at home through the
middle of the winter and not fishing at all. A modern name for him would
have been winter househusband!

When the children were older and more independent Gina went to work in a fine china shop in Palmerston Road and received good wages that helped meet the financial challenges that came with raising a family.

Figure 8: A sea bass catch aboard *Vanessa*, circa 1978

One day in the summer of 1970 Arthur was working near the Fairway buoy just outside the mouth of Langstone Harbour and his nets snagged what appeared to be a very old pewter tankard. Arthur took this piece to Bill Corney at Portsmouth City Museum (known today as Portsmouth Museum) to investigate its provenance. The tankard was sent to the Honourable Pewter Company where it was appraised as a fine, rare early seventeenth century Dutch example valued at £700.

Arthur sold the piece and the proceeds went in part to purchase a new SABB engine replacement for his boat. The balance of the sale money, in Arthur's words, *'went to finance further exploration'* as a friend of Arthur's had also found in the same area of the Solent a similar tankard of even greater value. He was convinced that a shipwreck with valuable artefacts must have gone down in the area centuries ago, and he held onto that belief for years to come.

Part II

The Find of a Lifetime

A Bad Day's Fishing

On the 5th May 1979 Arthur was out on the water with a friend, Melvin Gofton, in his fishing boat *Vanessa*. They were nearly four nautical miles southeast of Portsmouth in an area of the eastern Solent between Eastney and the Isle of Wight. Their trawl was set out behind the boat which moved ahead at slow speed. Suddenly and without warning the boat jerked to an abrupt stop – the net had caught on a seabed obstruction. They shipped the otter boards, put warps around the Samson post at the stern of the boat, and put the engine at full throttle to break the net free. This was successful and when the net was taken in a large square timber with wooden pegs called 'treenails' and corroded iron bolts were brought up. Arthur and Melvin took land transits so they could avoid the area in the future. It had been a bad day of fishing and all they had to show for it was a torn net that would be costly to repair. But Arthur's curiosity was stirred by the timber that had come up off the seabed.

> I took the timber home and became intrigued with it. I had a nagging feeling that there might be a very important wreck waiting to be found. I became so obsessed that I went out to the site in my own boat *Wishbone*. A chain was put between my two otter boards instead of a net and towed over the area. This I repeated for several days with no luck, but I still had the gut feeling there was a wreck. On the 15th of May I found it; my persistence had paid off. On the 27th of May I returned and secured an anchor and buoy to my trawl caught on the wreck, I retrieved my otter boards and went home. The next day I got in touch with my old friend and diver John Broomhead, along with Jim Boyle. We went out to the site in *Wishbone*, but a fast west-running tide was in full flow and the buoy was gone.

The story continues in John Broomhead's words. Recall from earlier in the story, in the 1950s Arthur had struck up a friendship with young John who worked in a local shop which purchased and resold Arthur's ragworm bait:

Figure 9: Arthur's fishing boat, aptly named *Wishbone*

One day in May, a local fisherman and lifelong friend Arthur Mack, saw me nosing about down at the small ferry boat terminal situated on the foreshore in Langstone Harbour. The ferry ride is a short crossing of a few hundred yards that carries passengers from Portsea Island out to what was at that time the idyllic Hayling Island.

I had not seen Arthur for some time, and he asked if I was still diving? He then explained that recently, whilst trawling with friend and fisherman Melvin Gofton in his fishing boat called Vanessa, they had caught their net on a solid seabed obstruction, known locally as a 'fastener'. He explained that they had used the power of the engine to rip the net free; when it was hauled back on board there was a large piece of timber tangled up in it. Now most fishermen would have sworn 'just a little' and cursed their ill luck before throwing the timber back over the side. However, in this instance, Arthur said that he 'had a feeling' about it and kept the timber. Bringing it ashore, he had stowed it under a small upturned rowboat on the foreshore alongside the ferry pontoon.

We made our way to the dingy in question and the timber he showed me was in fact two large pieces of oak in remarkably good condition, held together by several wooden pegs. Arthur, who never went to school, was made to work by his father to 'earn his keep' as a child. Despite this he had always held a fascination for history and especially old wooden ships. He will not mind me saying that at this time he could hardly read or write. Even so, he told me that the wooden pegs were known as 'treenails' and their presence indicated it was from something 'at least as old as the old girl herself'.

He was of course referring to Nelson's famous flagship, HMS *Victory*. He said that he had already asked other divers to have a look for him, but none were interested in something made of wood! Brass, copper, and lead being more the material to stir their interest. He then asked me if I would have a look for him because he said

'John, I have a feeling about this one. It is something very special.'

I will never forget those words 'I have a feeling' because they were to change the course of our lives. I told Arthur that I would be happy to have a look and asked if he could locate the snag again. After all, it was at night when he last snagged it and without leaving a marker buoy how would he find it again? He said

'John, I know almost exactly where it is.'

Arthur was so confident and enthusiastic about his 'feeling' that I got my diving gear and we did go out. It was a very relaxing, pleasant sunny day and life could not have been better. Unfortunately, we simply could not catch the gear on the wreck again on that day.

Not to be beaten, Arthur spent most of May in that year going out in the daytime, trawling up and down in the same area using a small otter trawl. On the 15th of May he hit the underwater obstruction again. Unfortunately, he would not leave his trawl gear out there with a buoy attached for fear of someone seeing it and stealing his net. On this occasion he was able to take his bearings in the daylight and Arthur assured us, he could 'definitely' snag the obstruction on the next trip! Although I had a nasty head cold and could not dive, friend & fellow diver Jim Boyle said he would come out and have a look. On May 28th in Arthur's little 16-foot open fishing boat, the three of us set off to find out just what it was on the seabed that kept snagging the net. We towed Arthur's trawling gear, which comprised of two small 'otter boards' with just chains joining them together. This allowed us to cover about 20 feet width of seabed on each pass over the approximate area where this unknown 'fastener' lay. Arthur, true to his word, hit the snag and Wishbone shuddered as she came to a sudden stop. With his huge piratical smile Arthur said, 'here we go'. Jim quickly got ready to go down and see what all the fuss was about, but just as he was about to go over the side into the water Arthur said to him 'go on then, it's not very deep – honest'. Jim was in the water for about 25 minutes before returning to the surface.

Back onboard *Wishbone* he confirmed that Arthur was being honest in saying 'it's not very deep' because at just 23 feet depth was the seabed. He also confirmed that the snag was indeed a line of very large wooden timbers but because the underwater visibility was so bad, he could see little else. Jim then took horizontal sextant readings; when these were plotted on an Admiralty chart it showed our position to be 50° 44 18 N / 01 01 36 W.

We had intended to go back as soon as possible but as was often the case, we could not find the wreck again mainly due to misty conditions making it impossible to see the land transit marks taken on the 28th.

Arthur's enthusiasm was infectious. So much so, that he persuaded me to go out with him when the tides and underwater visibility were better. Towards the end of May the weather forecast was favourable, and we were entering a period of neap tides. Plans were made and a date set for 1st June 1979 when we would dive and more seriously survey the wreck. Instead of wasting time towing trawling gear to find the snag Arthur went out the day before our planned dive to find and leave another marker on the wreck. Reluctantly, this time he left his trawling gear down there, marked with a large pink buoy in readiness for the day of the dive. This meant that in the event of not being able to see our landmarks we would be able to locate the spot again. To make doubly sure, in addition to the buoy on his trawl nets, he also snagged the obstruction with his grapple and left it there with a second marker buoy attached.

Due to business commitments Jim could not make it that day, and after collecting the diving gear with a couple of charged cylinders, together with another diving friend Steve Courtney, we set off to meet Arthur at his boat. On our approach along the narrow spit of land at Eastney leading out to ferry point, we saw Arthur's fishing boat, aptly named *Wishbone*, moored alongside the little wooden jetty. As we got close, we could hear the boat's single cylinder SABB diesel engine gently throbbing away. Arthur was sat in the stern waiting for us, clearly eager to be on his way to find out just what it was that kept calling him back to that same spot in the Solent. A spot halfway between Eastney beach, and Bembridge on the eastern corner of the Isle of Wight, off to the south.

As I recall the day was rather misty, lowering the land visibility to less than one mile. Remember that Wishbone was a small open fishing boat and did not have the luxury of a satellite navigation system or even a depth sounder for that matter! To find a position once offshore is purely down to the sighting and lining up of conspicuous landmarks. It took us an hour to get to the approximate area but by then the sea mist was so bad, we could not see the marker buoys left by Arthur the previous day. We motored around for a further half an hour when purely by chance, one of Arthur's bright pink buoys slowly appeared through the mist. I tell you now, it was spooky – just like seeing an eerie scene unfolding in an old swashbuckling pirate film. The tide was full on the ebb and running hard, which made diving almost impossible. However, by the time we had picked up the marker buoy, sorted the gear in readiness for the dive, it was nearing low tide and the associated slack water. This meant the tide race had slowed right down in readiness to change direction from ebb to flood. We had roughly half an hour in which to investigate this uncharted wreck that Arthur was so fired up about before the tide started flooding causing the tidal flow to increase once again.

We were approximately three miles out, well away from the harbour entrance we had left behind nearly two hours earlier. The land was obscured, as in every direction the glassy surface of the sea merged with the rolling sea mist. Diving under these conditions is always eerie and we were diving without life jackets which in hindsight was to say the least, 'a bit risky'. My dive log for the day shows that in a calm sea on a warm, sultry, summer's day we kitted up and quietly rolled over the side into the still water at 11.50 hours. Minutes later we reached the seabed at 26 feet depth. The underwater visibility was a reasonable 12 feet allowing us to see the timbers that Jim Boyle had mentioned after his dive of the previous month. The relatively shallow water at three miles from shore also indicated that we were right on top of the notorious wrecking area known as the Horse Tail sandbank, exactly as Arthur had suggested.

We set off along the wreckage feeling our way through thick kelp weed, stumbling across the remnants of several fishing nets snagged and abandoned on very substantial timbers. These timbers were in the region of 15 inches square and sticking out of the sand at an angle of about 40 degrees. There was only about an inch of clearance between each timber making it appear *like a row of gigantic teeth, stretching for what I estimated to be around 200 feet. The favourable weather conditions combined with good underwater visibility and very little tidal movement – what can I say – life could not have been better at that moment.*

On that first dive, Steve and I came across the remains of a large coil of rope lying on firm timber decking and lying at an angle relative to the seabed. Later in the project this rope was removed and identified as tarred hemp cable-laid rope in extremely good condition. The tidal flow started to pick up and strengthen rapidly, and within thirty minutes of feeling our way through the weed and around the wreckage it was time to make our way back to the light of day and the safety of Wishbone.

The three of us discussed the extent of the timbers upon which Arthur had inadvertently caught his nets on that fateful day. I was so impressed by the sheer enormity of the wreckage that my first words to him were to suggest that it all gave the impression of being the remains of a massive collapsed jetty or pier, and Steve agreed. This only added fuel to the fire already burning within Arthur and we formed an immediate 'secret' alliance to further investigate this underwater anomaly. We would do this when tidal conditions and underwater visibility were more favourable. We also agreed that not a word could be said to anyone about the find, until we knew exactly what it was.

By now the heat from the sun had lifted the sea mist and we could see land quite easily. We took some good land transit fixes from established marks to make future location of the site a little easier. These marks included one of the famous Solent Forts – Horse Sand Fort. The turret on top lined up exactly with the tall chimney at Fawley oil refinery, giving us the east-west transit line.

During the evening we transferred the transit marks onto our charts and plotted the position, which put us right in the middle of the Horse Tail sandbank. To the west there were several small wrecks ranging from modern sailing boats to an old MFV (Motor Fishing Vessel) that sank in the second war. To the north was the wreck of a dredger and less than a mile away to the east lay the remains of a German submarine UB21, one of my favourite wrecks for catching lobsters. A short distance to the south was the deep-water channel and several large modern wrecks. We discussed the events of the day over a beer and even before we ordered the second round of drinks, like

Arthur, I too was well and truly 'hooked' by the mystery and intrigue already starting to surround this unknown and uncharted large timber wreck.

My dive log for the day reads

'We carried out an initial survey of the wreck and found large wooden timber planks held together with wooden pegs. The bottom is loose sand and easily fanned aside, but quickly fills in if too large a hole is made. There is lead sheeting similar in size to floor tiles and several pieces of iron work.

Taken from wreck was:

Part of a leather shoe

Part of a steel shaft?

A piece of old wood with a peg through it'

Excavation & Investigation

With the discovery of a potentially historical find on their hands, there was no turning back from further pursuing the origin of the underwater curiosity. Whatever lay on the seabed captivated not only Arthur but John Broomhead as well, and this set both men on a path that would define the rest of their lives. The first order of business was to establish just what exactly had been found there upon the Horse Sands. John Broomhead explains further:

We started to get some idea of a possible origin of the wreck when on the 20th June 1979, just nineteen days after the first dive, I came across a large copper staple embedded in a flat timber. I managed to remove it and brought it to the surface for further investigation. Even though it had been worn away quite considerably by years of tidal erosion, a government 'Broad Arrow' mark was still clearly visible having been heavily stamped into the copper in antiquity. This gave us our first clue as to the original owners and what type of vessel we had found – a British naval ship, and a large one at that. An extract from my old dive log dated 27th June 1979 reads:

'Because of the evidence of the Broad Arrow on the copper staples, we suspect that the main wreckage is that of a British Man of War. The staples are very rough, and the broad arrow stamped on it indicating the wreck is possibly very old.'

We visited the site as often as possible over the next three months and I started keeping a far more accurate dive log and diary of events. We recovered many small objects that might possibly give us a clue as to the approximate date of the wreck. At this early stage in the project we had absolutely no excavation equipment whatsoever and all I could do was to fan away the sand using nothing more than my bare hands. This proved quite successful, provided the tidal stream was flowing at a steady rate. Clearly, with a wreck of this size we couldn't carry on any longer just fanning the sand with our hands! Using this method, one would equate the task to that of trying to plough a field with a teaspoon.

Arthur and John investigated how professional marine archaeologists undertook underwater excavations, and the equipment needed. The solution was an air lift – a long rigid tube extending between the surface of the water and the work site. Pumping compressed air down and releasing it through a nozzle inside the opening of the lift tube created suction that would draw seabed material up and be discharged away from the site. A diver/operator moves it about the excavation site as the work progresses. John built a homemade airlift while Arthur acquired an air pump which they fitted to the boat's engine – they were in business.

Whenever possible, we dived while the tide was flowing steadily in an easterly direction. This way, the debris taken up through the air lift was carried away downstream and away from the area of excavation. All debris tended to end up in a fairly limited area and the last job at the end of each day's diving was to go through the 'spoil heap' to make sure no small artefacts had accidentally been sucked up through the air lift.

With this new method of removing the seabed debris, another problem presented itself. The wreck is buried in loose sand and as quickly as I sucked sand away from a given area, the surrounding sand would be constantly trying to backfill it. Therefore, we would always try to find a wooden beam or some other solid object to act as a bulkhead against which to excavate. Of course, this problem was to stay with us for the duration of the project.

From the very start, the most difficult thing of all to deal with was the tide and weather. The wreck is situated on top of a shallow sand bank three miles offshore in the eastern Solent. On spring tides, due to the tremendous tidal flow that rips across the bank, it was impossible to dive. This effectively cut our window of diving opportunities by a third. Next, we were very reliant on the weather conditions. A wind of Force 5 or stronger hitting us from anywhere in the south-eastern quarter, met the easterly flowing tide causing a very uncomfortable 'short sea' over the bank. This made diving operations in such a small boat like Wishbone rather hazardous to say the least.

Artefacts recovered in the first few months of diving included hand grenades, flanged lead tubing, large copper staples, gun flints, musket shot, bones, a leather apron and other fragments, pottery sherds, broken bottles, shoes –

both complete and in pieces, a button, rigging blocks, and a sandglass for keeping time.

Looking at the evidence so far, all we really knew was that the objects told us we had found a naval ship. We carried out some research at the local library and positively dated the bottles to the mid-eighteenth century. The Portsmouth City Museum authorities said the pottery was of German origin and possibly dated sixteenth or seventeenth century. A quote from my diary from the end of June 1979 reads

'It is decided that it is about time we had an authority view the site and get further help. Accordingly, I telephoned Alexander McKee, and arranged an outing.'

The late Alexander McKee was a local historian living on Hayling Island and the man who first discovered and investigated the wreck of the Mary Rose in modern times. We shared with him our thoughts on the wreck. He asked if he could come along one day with us and see the wreck first-hand. On 25th July 1979, Alex and his wife Ilse came out with us in Wishbone and Jim Boyle gave him a guided tour over the wreck. Once back on Wishbone, Alex advised that he considered it to be far larger than the Mary Rose, in measuring the deck planks at 4 inches thick compared to 3 inches on the 'Rose. He said:

'She appears to have timber construction equal to that of Nelson's Flagship HMS Victory, which is a 1st rate ship of three decks.'

Soon afterward, with Alex having considered the circumstances, he was convinced that we had stumbled across the remains of HMS Impregnable – a 98-gun three-deck 2nd rate line of warship which sank in 1799. According to Alex, after his many years of researching historical wrecks in the Solent, this was the only ship lost in the area big enough to have timbers such as we had found on 'our' wreck.

Assembling a Project Team

The validation of the wreck being a large navy warship that came with Alexander McKee's assessment was of course met with excitement by Arthur and John. But this came with an awareness that any future undertakings at the wreck site were going to be greater in scale and execution than either man could have envisioned at the outset of the project. The work looming ahead eclipsed both men's abilities and resources, and so they came to the realisation that assembling a team of professionals would be essential for a successful endeavour. John Broomhead continues:

> *Having registered the find with the Receiver of Wreck on 16th August 1979, it was time for archaeological advice. Our first instinct was to approach the Curator of the Royal Naval Museum, Commander Gregory Clark, MBE, BA, Royal Navy (Ret'd) to ask his advice on who best to seek and call upon for guidance. After all, the Broad Arrow marks on everything had already shown us that we were dealing with an Admiralty ship. The local renowned archaeologist and obvious choice was Margaret Rule, but at that time she was totally consumed with the Mary Rose project and we felt that we deserved someone who could afford us a lot of time. We also wanted an experienced person who could help unlock some of the mysteries already surrounding the artefacts, for we were still convinced that the identification of the wreck lay in these fascinating items we had recovered from the seabed.*

Arthur and John made an appointment to visit the Royal Naval Museum in Portsmouth Dockyard. With the two men sitting in his office and having heard the story of their find, Commander Clark placed a call to Commander John M. Bingeman who had extensive diving experience on and archaeological oversight for the historic wreck sites of the *Assurance* (1753) and *Pomone* (1811). Commander Bingeman suggested that Arthur and John meet with him straightaway to discuss their discovery, which today he reflects on *'as one of the best decisions I have ever made in my life'*. Within a half hour of meeting, Arthur and John had arrangements with him to visit and dive the wreck, which occurred on 5th April 1980:

> *I took John out for a good look around the site. After the dive, whilst sat in Wishbone anchored above the wreck, we agreed to form a partnership and apply for a Wreck Protection Order. John said that in all the wrecks he had dived around the world this was not only the largest but had the promise of being the most exciting. Now we had another team member on board with us. During 1980 John Bingeman and I dived on the wreck as often as possible and recovered a large quantity and variety of artefacts.*

> *On 10th April 1980, policewoman and keen scuba diver Sandy Blake joined the dive team to work the wreck. I gave her a guided tour of the site and she expressed her fascination in everything she had seen. Making our way back along the shot line she pointed to a small, rectangular-shaped bit of material poking out of the sand amongst some broken timbers. It was a piece of leather approximately 9 inches long by 4 inches wide [Figure 10] which we recovered and took back to the dive boat. Subsequent research identified that it was part of a shot cartridge case and remarkably, there was a King's monogram embossed very clearly on one side. More importantly, it had the numeral '2' embossed within the letter G, beneath the crown. At last, an accurate date to go by. King George II had reigned from 1727 to 1760. A big 'well done!' to Sandy – this was the most important artefact found to date!*

Figure 10: Leather cartridge case found on the *Invincible* wreck

In the spring of 1980 divers carried out a pre-disturbance survey of the wreck and John Bingeman completed the application for a

Government Protection Order. Dr Margaret Rule had volunteered to be the project's archaeological advisor, and Mr Christopher O'Shea in-charge of the Portsmouth City Museums' Conservation Laboratory, had agreed to be the official conservation officer. The Advisory Committee for Historic Wreck Sites accepted the application and recommended the Secretary of State to grant a licence which was issued on the 30th September 1980 as 'Site Number 22'. It was a remarkable achievement for the team.

John Broomhead's recollection of site work in the second year of the project continues:

Artefacts found during the excavations included many pulley blocks of different types and sizes, but one remains embedded in my memory to this day. I was diving with John Bingeman and Norman Bradburn on 12th July 1980, when we recovered what I originally called an 'inline double pulley block'. It was huge and it clearly had a specific purpose but at the time I had no idea what it might be. After bringing it to the surface, I took it home with me to photograph for my records. To give an idea of its scale and size, this image [Figure 11] shows the block, which was later identified to be a 'Fiddle Block', stood up alongside my then two-year old daughter Jaime.

Other artefacts found in those early days of the project included a variety of silver and gilt numbered Army uniform buttons. We had found numbered buttons for the 13th, 14th, 24th, 30th, 43rd, 59th, and 64th Regiments of foot soldiers. We were convinced that the buttons would give us a clue as to the identity of the wreck. Why had we found so many different numbered regimental buttons on the wreck? Is it possible that a campaign in history featured all these regiments? If there was such a campaign, then were the troops transported overseas in a vessel that foundered before it even left the confines of the Solent?

Our efforts were not limited to underwater excavation work on the wreck site. Many hours were spent in the Public Records Office and naval document archives trying to find more clues as to the name of the ship. The artefacts were giving us dates of between the late sixteenth and late eighteenth centuries which was not conclusive by any means. Commander Bingeman also endeavoured to make the most of his status as an officer in the Royal Navy, and investigations were initiated within the Admiralty.

Figure 11: Jaime Broomhead and an *Invincible* rigging block, 1980

With the perceived date range, and consideration for the size of the timbers on the wreck site, there was strong opinion that we had found the Invincible – an eighteenth century 3rd rate warship originally captured from the French at the Battle of Cape Finisterre in May 1747, named L'Invincible. According to record she was brought back to Portsmouth and put straight into British service with the name Invincible. However, there were significant flaws in this theory:

1. *Among the artefacts recovered to date were a few gun 'rammer' heads. Used for tamping the shot down the muzzle of a gun during battle, they were stamped with the size of gun for which they were intended. We found them for 9, 24 & 32 pounder guns. However, the original manifest for Invincible showed her to have sizes 9, 18 & 32 pounder guns. And so, you see there was an anomaly in the gun battery on the upper deck.*

2. *According to all Army, Navy and other governmental records, the numbered regimental buttons we were finding on the wreck did not come into existence until 1768, and the Invincible had sunk some ten years earlier in 1758.*

Figure 12: Arthur & John Bingeman examining wreck artefacts

I stated earlier that fishermen live mainly on their luck – well Arthur is particularly lucky. He was convinced that we had found the wreck of the Invincible. Two members of our slowly growing team, John Bingeman & David Houghton, went to the Records Office at Priddy's Hard Armament Depot at Gosport. In amongst many hundreds of old records going back well into the beginning of the eighteenth century they found a number of letters relating to Invincible including one dated 23rd December 1755 from the Office of Ordnance – the first sentence reads

'Gentlemen

I am Commanded by the Board to acquaint you that His Majesty's Ship Invincible is for the future to be Gunn'd with 24 pounders upon her Upper Deck instead of the 18 pounders as desired by the Lords of the Admiralty...'

This shows just how important research was to the project. Soon after this Arthur, who was by then the team's research director, found an extract from the log of the Dublin – a navy warship that had been moored in the lee of the Isle of Wight at the time of the Invincible's demise. The Dublin was in a sorry state of repair and unable to put to sea, and from the log written and signed by Captain Rodney (later to become Admiral Rodney) a sentence read

'This day we did witness the destruction of Invincible, ashore upon the Deans Sands'

Proof positive came on the 30th May 1981 when excavating within the Forward Sail Room of the ship, John Bingeman came across a wooden tally stick wrapped within a fragment of sail, and written on it were the words 'Invincible Flying Jib 26.26 No 6' – one of the ship's sails.

Throughout all this Arthur remained 'topside' on the dive boat when the team was working the wreck site. Day after day he would see ship's timbers, gear and other artefacts surfacing with the excavation team. He felt as though he was missing out diving with them and seeing these incredible finds first-hand. However, Arthur bearing a streak of superstition for such things as weather and karma, as perhaps most fishermen do, maintained that because of *'all the enemies I must have down there, perhaps I should not risk going underwater in the Solent'*. Nonetheless Arthur cast his reservations aside and called upon his colleagues to teach him how to scuba dive. Arthur admits that beforehand

Without telling anyone, I decided to fill the bath & after putting on a snorkel and mask I laid under the water to see if I could breath and not panic. I found that I could...

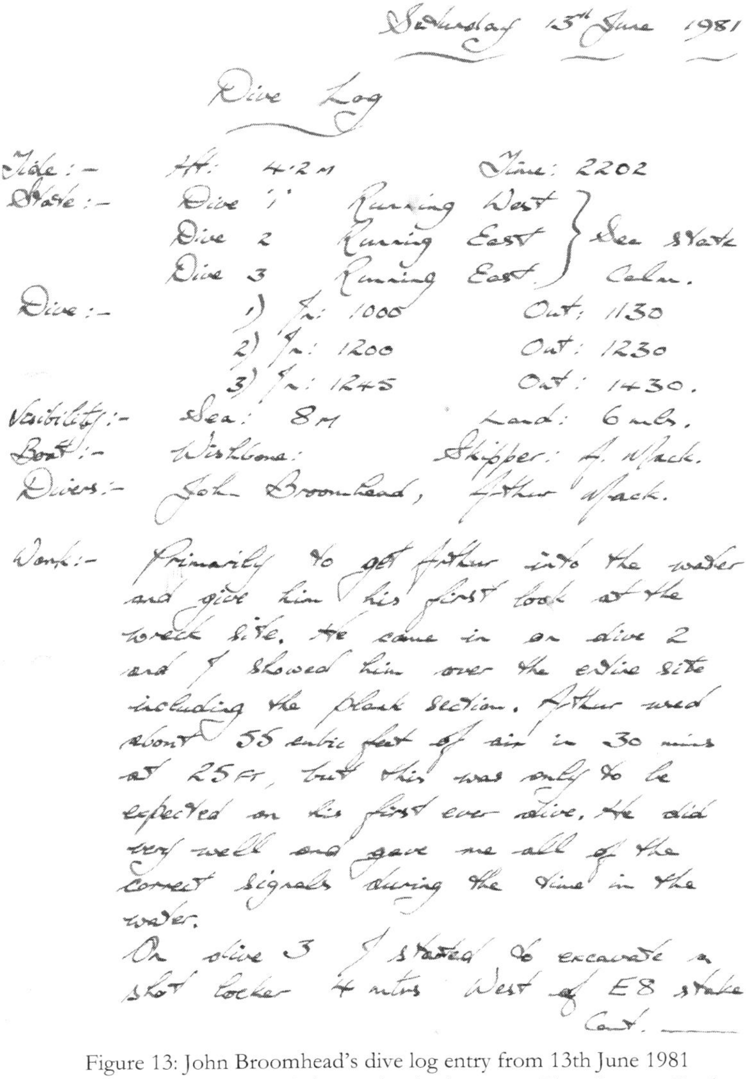

Saturday 13th June 1981

Dive Log

Tide :–   Ht: 4·2 m   Time: 2202
State :–   Dive 1 Running West ⎤
           Dive 2 Running East ⎬ Sea State
           Dive 3 Running East ⎦ Calm.
Dive :–   1) In: 1000   Out: 1130
                 2) In: 1200   Out: 1230
                 3) In: 1245   Out: 1430.
Visibility:– Sea: 8 m   Land: 6 mls.
Boat :–   Wishbone: Skipper: A. Mack.
Divers:– John Broomhead, Arthur Mack.

Work:– Primarily to get Arthur into the water
and give him his first look at the
wreck site. He came in on dive 2
and I showed him over the entire site
including the plank section. Arthur used
about 55 cubic feet of air in 30 mins
at 25 ft, but this was only to be
expected on his first ever dive. He did
very well and gave me all of the
correct signals during the time in the
water.
On dive 3 I started to excavate a
shot locker 4 mtrs West of E8 stake
                                    Cont.

Figure 13: John Broomhead's dive log entry from 13th June 1981

The Naval Sub-Aqua Club took Arthur to Pitt Street Baths in Landport where, beginning in 1910, all Royal Navy recruits were sent to learn how to swim; at that time it was known as the Royal Naval School of Physical Training. Arthur managed fine and by early summer of 1981 he was ready to venture into the deep. John Broomhead took Arthur down on the wreck site for the first time on 13th June 1981. John recalls that Arthur used a significant amount of breathing gas in a relatively short time, but this was entirely to be expected. The stress of being in an open and dynamic sea environment, coupled with poor visibility, as compared to the confined safety and security of a swimming pool, will cause anxiety and rapid breathing in almost anyone. John's diving log from that day summarises the event [Figure 13].

Figure 14: John Broomhead & Arthur (right) excavating the wreck

Arthur continued and with each dive he gained increasing confidence and skill. He was down on the wreck often with the other divers in the team, assisting with surveying and using the airlift as part of the excavation work. He eventually reached a point that he no longer cared to participate, and instead focused on working the dive boat, and back on land would engage in archival research and artefact conservation as other ways to support the project.

Saga of the *Invincible*

The *Invincible* had become stranded on the Dean Sand, known today as Horse Tail, after a calamitous series of events upon weighing anchor early in the morning of 19th February 1758. The *Invincible* was one amongst a fleet of British warships and troop transports assembled at St. Helen's Roads – a Navy anchorage off the Isle of Wight's northeast coast. The fleet, commanded by Admiral Edward Boscawen, was readying to sail across the Atlantic to Nova Scotia in Canada for the planned capture of French-held Fortress Louisbourg. This was to be the second expedition to Canada after the first attempt undertaken the year before met with disaster – the fleet was hit by a hurricane off Nova Scotia and many ships including *Invincible* were damaged. The plan to capture Louisbourg would be the first step in destroying their enemy's foothold in North America so that Britain could affirm political dominance and protect its economic interests vested in the territory.

In its time the *Invincible* was revered as the Royal Navy's fastest and best performing warship, but these virtues were not to the credit of British ship designers. The vessel had been built by the French Navy in a shipbuilding yard at Rochefort in the south west of France and was launched there in 1744. The English soon took notice of this new, impressive, and rather large 74-gun ship. Admiral George Anson recognised *L'Invincible* as a fine instrument of war and coveted her. When opportunity arose at the Battle of Cape Finisterre on 14th May 1747, Anson seized his chance and captured the ship as a war prize. It was escorted back to Britain and received at Portsmouth Dockyard for survey, repairs, and refitting as a British ship-of-the-line. From that point in history onward the *Invincible* has always been associated with Portsmouth, her home port.

It was soon discovered that the ship's design was nothing like British Establishment, and the ship proved herself to be technically and operationally superior to any other vessel of similar rating in the Royal Navy. We know today that eighteenth century French naval administrators placed significant emphasis on engineering and science in ship design, whereas their British counterparts were limited by established 'best practices' that employed empirical methodology (design improvisation by trial & error) rather than systematic theory. Ten years after *Invincible's* capture, Anson had finally persuaded the Admiralty of this French design superiority and new English-built ships were adopting *Invincible's* lines.

Figure 15: *His Majesty's Ship Invincible* by R. Short, 1751

By the Battle of Trafalgar in 1805, nearly 75 per cent of the Royal Navy's fleet comprised so-called 3rd rate 74-gun ships based on *Invincible's* lines. As Arthur stated in one of his papers, 'the future dominance of the Royal Navy was significantly influenced by the technology of Britain's fiercest competitor, France.'[6]

The accidental loss of *Invincible* in February 1758 resonated through the Navy; a concerted but unsuccessful effort was initially made to save the ship. After the vessel was declared a loss the Navy Board issued a public tender in the hope of securing a viable plan to raise it off the seabed and move the wreck into dock for repairs, for which no satisfactory proposal was submitted. Realising that *Invincible's* fate had been sealed on the Dean Sand, a salvage operation to remove and reuse the ship's equipment and stores was undertaken in the summer of 1758. Eventually the remains of the ship disappeared, entombed by sand and sea. When Arthur found the wreck 221 years later, he was at the right place at the right time. The sandbank had migrated so that the wreck protruded from the seabed – lying in wait for Arthur's happenstance encounter.

Figure 16: *Invincible stranded on Sunday 19th February 1758* by John R. Terry

Two concerted efforts were spearheaded in unison by Arthur and the project team: a decade-long underwater archaeological programme to excavate and document the wreck and recover its artefacts, and, comprehensive archival research to establish the history of the ship and the circumstances which lead to her loss. The formal recognition that came with the government designating *Invincible* as a Protected Wreck on 30th September 1980 brought significant pride to the team – the wreck was now identified as a National Monument and a facet of the United Kingdoms' underwater heritage. Furthermore, the *Invincible* was recognised as bridging a chronological gap in British warship design between *Mary Rose* and *HMS Victory*.

Indeed, the *Victory* greatly benefited from the discovery of the *Invincible*. The ship's Grand Magazine, where gunpowder was stored in the fore hold of the ship, is patterned from that which was identified on the *Invincible* wreck. Until it had been found no surviving example existed that explained how the magazine on a 'ship-of-the-line' was fitted in the latter part of the eighteenth century. At the time of its recovery from the wreck the historical importance of the magazine timbers was not initially appreciated, and they were almost discarded. Recognising their intrinsic value, Arthur argued for them to be salvaged and conserved, and the surviving portion of *Invincible's* magazine was reassembled at the Historic Dockyard Chatham. When Peter Goodwin, past Keeper and Curator of *HMS Victory*, needed to reconstruct the *Victory's* long-since removed Grand Magazine, he examined and measured the *Invincible* display at Chatham. Further applying archival research, details of *Invincible's* magazine enabled Goodwin to generate designs for an authentic reproduction with the *Victory*. More than this, the construction found in *Invincible* provided measurements for the racking on which gun powder cartridges were stored. Consequent to this, authentic racking was similarly designed and reintroduced into *Victory's* two ready use hanging magazines as well, thereby completing the interpretation of gunpowder cartridge storage in the ship. Today these displays, seen by more than half a million visitors entering the *Victory* every year, is very much accredited to Arthur.

Also much added to Arthur's recognition are the host of *Invincible* relics which equally enabled Peter Goodwin to provide detailed interpretation throughout the *Victory,* especially on matters related to gunnery equipment. The gunpowder barrels on display in the Grand Magazine are reproductions of *Invincible* artefacts, for which no original examples existed previously. Some 48 barrels – intact and still full of gunpowder – were excavated from the wreck. Cylindrical 'cases of wood' were used to carry made-up cartridge bags of powder charge from the magazines up to the gun decks; copies patterned on ones from the *Invincible* can be seen throughout *Victory.*

On the domestic issues of shipboard life, replica square wooden trenchers (simple wooden plates), utensils and wooden tankards based on those recovered from the *Invincible* wreck site, added interpretation. As Goodwin stated, *'As an historical source aiding the Victory's interpretation, Arthur's Invincible proved endlessly unique'.*

Figure 17: Arthur with *Invincible* artefacts aboard *HMS Victory* – early 1980s

The first public promotion of the *Invincible* Project was a window display of *Invincible* artefacts in one of Portsmouth Dockyard's Georgian-era Storehouses, seen by many visitors on their way to the Royal Naval Museum and *HMS Victory*. On 8th April 1981, this display was officially opened by Rear Admiral Tippet – Flag Officer Portsmouth, Captain Livesay – Commanding Officer of the 6th *Invincible* which had only recently been commissioned, and members of the project team. Four months later an August weekend show was held in Southsea where all the project members and even Gina took turns overseeing a display of *Invincible* artefacts.

In 1984 the Project produced a travelling exhibition intent on educating the public on the significance of the *Invincible* as one of the most influential ships of the Royal Navy in the era of King George II. It was decided that the exhibit needed a spokesperson who could promote and draw the attention necessary to make it a success. One evening Arthur was at home watching television and happened upon a programme featuring the *SS Great Britain*. The documentary included an appearance by Robin Gibb of the pop music band the *Bee Gees*, himself a history enthusiast and proponent of England's maritime heritage. From this Arthur had the idea of proposing that Robin Gibb should be invited to be the project's spokesperson. It seemed improbable to the team they could secure someone with such serious 'star-power' – nonetheless the effort was set in motion and Mr Gibb's publicity agent, Felicity Hatton, was contacted. Days later she replied to John Broomhead with the news that Mr Gibb was interested, and he ultimately put his support behind the venture.

The exhibition launch took place on Monday, 4th June 1984 at the Hospitality Inn, Southsea, amid significant media coverage. Mr Ainsley Adams, a professional photographer who specialised in covering local-icon musicians in the Southampton area in the 1970s through the mid-1980s, was hired to photograph the event and its celebrity guest. After Robin Gibb's opening speech, he spoke with the team to congratulate them on the success of their endeavour, particularly for the excavation work and conservation of artefacts, for which they had no funding support. Arthur remembers Gibb as *'a very pleasant and easy to talk to person – it was a pleasure to meet him'*. A bit later in the event someone noticed that both Gibb and Arthur had left the venue. He asked Arthur how he had come to find the *Invincible* and Arthur offered to show him in person. They left the hotel and walked down to Southsea beach, where Arthur pointed out the location of *Invincible* in the Solent some three miles to the south. After hearing Arthur's story of stumbling on the wreck, Gibb said he must be a 'very lucky man'. Arthur recalls

Figure 18: Robin Gibb opening the *Invincible* Exhibition

I grinned and showed Robin the gold snake ring I was wearing and told him the story of how I'd found it. He couldn't believe it.

The tale of Arthur finding the ring is presented later in the story. The exhibition was an instant success because of Robin Gibb's support. It remained there for two months, after which it was moved to its first hired display at Chichester District Museum.

Figure 19: Robin Gibb & Arthur with an *Invincible* artefact

In 1986 Arthur and Gina went on a trip to France with Gina's brother, Thomas Shepherd. They visited Rochefort, a port on the Charente estuary and site of one of the country's most important naval dockyards. It was here between 1741 and 1744 that *L'Invincible* was built, launched, and commissioned into the French Navy. This was a memorable trip for Arthur, to see the very dock where the *Invincible* had been built – it provided him with a sense of completeness to the storied history of the ship. He gave to the National Marine Museum at Rochefort an *Invincible* artefact recovered by the team – a parrel truck, which is a piece associated with the ship's masts and spars.

In 1989 a national exhibit of *Invincible* artefacts was opened by Lord Carrington with the firing of a cannon at Historic Dockyard Chatham to open the *'Wooden Walls'* exhibition. Arthur is quite proud of having a discussion with Lord Carrington at the opening ceremony, concerning the importance of the *Invincible* as it served to mature and refine British warship design in the latter half of the eighteenth century.

Figure 20: The dock where *Invincible* was built

The *Invincible* story did not end with Arthur and the team. Several books and academic manuscripts have been published, broadening the knowledge of the ship and her history among scientists, archaeologists, historians, and enthusiasts alike. Today, ongoing excavation and study of the wreck has uncovered a treasure trove of artefacts, new information concerning the design and construction of the ship, and a clearer understanding of what happened to *Invincible* after she was lost. The *Invincible* exhibit at Historic Dockyard

Chatham lives on today as part of the new *'Command of the Oceans'* multi-gallery installation with a superb expanded display of some of *Invincible's* most interesting and impressive artefacts – including the original Grand Magazine saved by Arthur. A new exhibition entitled *'Diving Deep: HMS Invincible 1744'* dedicated to the story of the *Invincible*, has been developed by the National Museum of the Royal Navy. Its modular design allows elements of the display to tour the country after the launch at Chatham and Portsmouth.

Arthur's discovery and accomplishments associated with the *Invincible* never inflated his ego or altered his character, despite the attention and credit he deservedly acquired. In his own understated manner Arthur quips

Twice I was invited by the Captain of the most recent line of ships to be named Invincible to dine onboard. On the first occasion I was somewhat baffled by the array of cutlery and its use.

This reference is to the sixth such ship in the history of the Royal Navy to bear the name *Invincible* and one of the most well-known warships of recent times, having served in the Falkland War in 1982.

Figure 21: 1st *Invincible* wreck buoy, the project team's dive boat *Ceres*, and the 6th *Invincible* beyond, 1984

The Project and the company formed by the team, *Invincible Conservations (1744-1758) Limited* continued until 1991. During those years Arthur still managed to do some fishing when time permitted. It was more out of necessity than choice, as there were no profits associated with the project and rather the opposite, as especially in the early days the site work investigations and equipment were funded by the team itself. Throughout this endeavour Arthur had the unwavering support of his family at home. According to Arthur, Gina never questioned his pursuit of the *Invincible* – after all it was Arthur's lifelong ability to find things, beginning in his childhood and continuing later in life as a career fisherman, which supported the family. As for their children, Arthur says *'they all thought I was crackers looking for pieces of old wood. However, they knew that I was born lucky at finding things of interest but never expected one of my finds to be a large ship.'*

Other Maritime Pursuits

Throughout the *Invincible* Project Arthur took on other opportunities to support his livelihood and to further his interests in history, archaeology, and self-study.

In September 1983 Arthur was invited to assist John Bingeman and the Portsmouth RN Sub-Aqua Club (BSAC Special Branch 749) to recover a bronze minion – a type of small-bore cannon – found just outside Yarmouth Harbour on the Isle of Wight. It was found on the wreck of a Renaissance Period vessel which may have been the Spanish ship *Santa Lucia*, lost in 1567 en route to Flanders with a cargo of wool.[7] The gun is believed to have been cast by Giovanni (Zuane) Alberghetti, a prominent Venetian gun founder of the sixteenth century.

Arthur carried on with his fishing career until 1987. In 1982 the Ministry of Agriculture and Fisheries banned fishing in all harbours, citing they were important breeding grounds for many species of fish. This was a huge upset to all in the fishing industry who worked those waters, and Arthur was no exception. Furthermore, the Ministry also began increasing the minimum size of the fish that could be kept from a catch. This applied to sea bass which was Arthur's primary source of income and made it difficult for him to earn a living. These circumstances ultimately pushed Arthur out of the career, yet in the bigger picture he has no regrets:

Regrets for fishing full time? Not really! When I think about it, I would never have found the wreck of the Invincible! You could easily say that finding the wreck was the start of my education. I learned a lot about reading and writing and my vocabulary increased considerably as a result. It must also be said that by finding the Invincible, I got to know and meet many nice people from all walks of life, from all over the world.

Despite the setback, around the same time a new opportunity arose as work continued with the *Invincible* Project. In 1987 Arthur became a paid employee of *Invincible Conservations (1744-1758) Limited* and worked alongside Simon Aked in the conservation laboratory. Arthur found this valuable not only from the perspective of caring for the ship's artefacts to ensure their long-term integrity and survival, but also from an academic perspective in that he acquired new technical knowledge and skill.

Other work prospects came about for Arthur at the end of 1987 when John Bingeman established Bingeman Marine Services Limited. The company contracted various local jobs and Arthur often worked with John as his associate. After the 'Great Storm of 1987' which hit the nation in mid-October, Arthur and John salvaged yachts and other boats that had sunk or been washed ashore on Portsea Island and surrounding areas. Other contracts which Arthur collaborated in were the installation and maintenance of laneways and marker buoys for Strongman competitions, windsurfing off Southsea; and water skiing and other water sport activities off Lee-on-Solent further west.

Figure 22: Arthur & John Bingeman in *Wishbone*

The company was retained by the Mary Rose Trust to assist in setting up underwater wood deterioration tests to monitor timber degradation on the *Grace Dieu* (1439), *Invincible* (1758) and *Hazardous* (1706) wreck sites. Another endeavour Arthur took part in alongside John was the television production *Dirty Weekend* – a programme on the state of pollution in the Solent and how it impacted marine recreational activities in the Portsmouth area. A television broadcasting company hired out John's boat *Viney Peglar* for filming in and around Portsmouth Harbour; Arthur was boatman in John's 'crew'. Arthur participated in these and other small projects, often with the use of his own boat *Wishbone*, until 2010.

In March 1991, the Society for Nautical Research (South) bestowed upon Arthur the Bill Majer Memorial Fund annual award, so named in honour of the Society's founder and first Chairman; he later became President holding office from 1980 to 1987. The award recognised Arthur's contribution to *A Comparison of French and British Naval Shipbuilding in the 18th Century,* for which he produced a paper that attributed reasons for the shortcomings in the design of British warships relative to their French counterparts. In his research Arthur investigated numerous archival and contemporary sources to persuasively establish root cause – ineffectual shipbuilding tradition, ignorance of science and mathematics, and short-sighted policy and practice within the mandate of the Navy Board. Arthur's paper was subsequently published in *Flagship* – The Journal of the World Ship Trust, Marine Society, London, in October 1992. In 1995 his research and findings concerning French influence on the design of British frigates were received by author Robert Gardiner as contributing content in his two-volume publication *The Heavy Frigate: Eighteen-Pounder Frigates: 1778-1800.*

Arthur's studies have also included a significant investment of time researching the development of British Army regiments from the beginning of the eighteenth century onward to the time of *Invincible's* loss in the Solent in February 1758. When the ship went aground, she was carrying Army personnel, equipment and supplies to Canada and elsewhere in North America at the height of Britain's fight for colonial dominance. The excavation of the *Invincible* wreck throughout the 1980s revealed many numbered buttons originating from regimental uniforms. This was a revelation soon to become embroiled in controversy and challenged by historians and academics alike, as contemporary opinion believed that regiments did not identify their uniforms with representative numbering until after the Royal Clothing Warrant of 1767. The research undertaken by Arthur provided compelling evidence to the contrary, and in 1997 Arthur and John had an associated manuscript published in *The International Journal of Nautical Archaeology*.

Another of Arthur and John Bingeman's exploits involved the examination and scrutiny of approximately ten tons of copper sheathing removed from *HMS Victory* during ongoing repairs and restorative work to the ship. The intent of this review was to document manufacturers' names and inspectors' marks associated with the supply of sheathing to all the Navy's warships – a practice which was introduced in the latter half of the eighteenth century to protect ships' wooden hulls from deterioration caused by 'ship worm'. Identifying this information provided historical insight into the times throughout the ship's service when *Victory* was sheathed, and specific materials information including sheet gauge and alloy composition which evolved and advanced over time. With assistance from John Bethell and support from Peter Goodwin, Arthur and John published a paper in *The International Journal of Nautical Archaeology* in the year 2000. A selection of copper sheets from this project are on display in The National Waterfront Museum in Swansea, loaned by the National Museum of the Royal Navy.

It is evident that after Arthur retired from fishing, he reinvented himself through self-education and contributed to a number of academically recognised achievements. Arthur was just beginning his adventures in archaeology, with more history-changing finds awaiting him.

Figure 23: Arthur alongside the *Hazardous* (1706) wreck buoy

Part III

Still in the Mud

Ancient Finds in Langstone Harbour

In the span of at least six decades Arthur has spent a great amount of time sleuthing around the foreshore of Langstone Harbour, a 5000-acre body of water lying in between the islands of Portsea and Hayling on Hampshire's south coast. It is believed to have once been a river valley of one of several tributaries that flowed into what was then the River Solent. Sometime between 4,000 and 3,500 BC it became a saltwater bay as sea levels rose after the last ice age.[8]

Arthur continued fishing, bait collecting and oyster gathering in Langstone Harbour into the 1990s but more for the benefit of his recreation and leisure than work. He would often go out alone or sometimes with a friend and walk the mud flats at low tide, scanning for anything of interest exposed by low water and natural erosive actions at work.

Over the years Arthur's investigations and exploits in Langstone have yielded a vast array of finds from many different time periods throughout history. The islands in the northern area of the harbour – North & South Binness, Long and Baker's Islands – have yielded many a fascinating artefact found and collected by Arthur. His oldest finds from there are flint cutting tools, axe and spear heads dated to 10,000 years which correlates to the Upper Palaeolithic period of the Stone Age. The eroding ledges of the northern islands have also uncovered Mesolithic (beginning in 7,000 BC; a time when Britain was still connected to mainland Europe) and Neolithic (4,000-3,500 BC) flint artefacts. The Neolithic period in Britain represents a time when inhabitants were transitioning from hunting and gathering to farming which eventually included the raising of livestock. In his familiarity with the artefacts recovered in and around Langstone Harbour, the academic knowledge he has gained through working alongside professional archaeologists, and his self-studies, Arthur believes that Long Island has been inhabited for thousands of years and likely housed permanent settlements in prehistoric times.

Figure 24: Selsey Bill (top), Hayling Island and Portsea Island

Arthur has also observed a significant quantity of domestic earthenware pottery and sherds classified as Early Bronze Age circa 2,000 BC and Samian ware that is indicative of Roman-era habitation in Britain (AD 43-410). Langstone Harbour is well represented by a wealth of Bronze Age (2,500-800 BC) artefacts: flint knives, arrow heads, a torq (neck ring), a quern stone (for grinding cereals and other harvested or gathered foods), fire hearths and kilns, remnants of animal pens, and a grouping of funerary urns containing cremated human remains – among other relics.

Partnership in Archaeology

The discovery of a cluster of fossilised tree stumps in the northern reaches of Langstone Harbour, first made by Arthur in the 1970s whilst bait digging, would later become one of his most prolific discoveries. Determined to prove his find to professional archaeologists, he relocated those remains – a prehistoric submerged forest – in 1995 while working with Wessex Archaeology. The firm recognised the find as having significance to the history of coastal change in the south of England. On both occasions the discoveries occurred in extreme low tide conditions; in other words – normally submerged and hidden from view. Radiocarbon dating of the oak, yew, willow, and alder specimens implied the remains were Neolithic, marking ingression of the sea into Langstone Harbour and altering it from a freshwater delta to a saltwater bay of the Solent. Traces of burnt flint and charcoal found in the peat surrounding the tree remains proved the area was inhabited by humans dating back some 6,000 years ago, before being submerged by the sea. In April 2000, *The Newsletter of The Prehistoric Society, 'PAST'*, published by University College London reported these findings and cited Arthur's role in Wessex Archaeology's study. Arthur relates his association:

> *In 1991, Hampshire County Council financed an archaeological survey of Langstone Harbour. Michael Hughes was the County Archaeologist employed by Wessex Archaeology and who was based in Salisbury and associated with both Portsmouth and Southampton Universities. Because of my detailed knowledge of the harbour and its archaeology I was approached by the Hampshire & Wight Trust for Maritime Archaeology, based at the National Oceanography Centre at the University of Southampton, to take part in the survey. Since I had been collecting artefacts from the harbour for over forty years, I was able to take the archaeologists, in my boat, to places where I had previously found artefacts. I could also show them sites on the shore where I had found archaeological material. This was invaluable since the survey was restricted, because of nesting sea birds, to the second week of August.*

The intent of the Langstone Harbour Archaeological Survey project,

was a multidisciplinary study of the prehistoric to early-historic use and development of what is now a large, shallow, marine inlet on the south coast of England. Its main objectives were to survey and record the archaeology within the harbour itself and of its immediate hinterland and to determine its physical, environmental, and social development.[9]

The seven-year project involved the undertaking of a variety of fieldwork survey methods including scuba diving, so called 'walkover' and 'swimover' investigations, auger sampling, and geo-mapping. Access throughout the harbour was hampered and challenged by natural conditions, being an intertidal zone comprised of marshland and mud flats with clays, organic materials, and saturated, loose soils.

Figure 25: Arthur with survey equipment on Long Island

The team relied heavily on Arthur's extensive knowledge of local artefact finds, site conditions and accessibility of the Harbour, and without his guidance they may not have realised the success achieved.

The outcome of the fieldwork and academic study was comprehensive mapping and evaluation of recorded artefacts and historical features including submerged ancient forests, wrecks, wooden and other non-timber structures, buried human remains in funerary urns, fire hearths and kilns, animal bones, worked flint, hand tools, and pottery. Upon conclusion of the study, a research report authored by Michael J. Allen and Julie Gardiner entitled *Our Changing Coast: A survey of the intertidal archaeology of Langstone Harbour, Hampshire* was published in 2000 by the Council for British Archaeology.

Figure 26: Arthur & Michael J. Allen celebrating the publication of *Our Changing Coast*

Arthur did not merely assist in the fieldwork but was also recognised as a principal contributor, having authored content regarding his discoveries of the 'Sinah Circle structure' and 'Little Rock Leak' stones. The Report's Dedication reads

for
Richard Bradley and Arthur Mack
professional and amateur alike
who have shown a passion for the past of Langstone Harbour

Throughout the 1990s Arthur had engaged in a partnership agreement with both the University of Portsmouth and the University of Southampton wherein he took students of Archaeology out in his boat *Wishbone* on excursions around Langstone Harbour, to view the locations of historically significant artefact finds in the area. He enjoyed the opportunity to share his knowledge with young people who were embarking on a career as professional archaeologists.

Sinah Circle Structure

The lowest local tide of the twentieth century occurred on 16th March 1993 due to high barometric pressure with easterly gales blocking the tide and holding it down the English Channel. Arthur and his friend John Male had taken advantage of the low water conditions and were out oyster gathering in Sinah Lake, a minor channel in the south-eastern reaches of Langstone Harbour.

In this area, which would normally be submerged by about 10 feet of seawater at high tide, they came across a collection of 27 upstanding wood stumps laid out in a circular arrangement some 21 feet in diameter on what appeared to be a low-elevated mud bank. Arthur contacted his colleague and friend John Bingeman to discuss the find, and the two decided it was imperative to conduct a survey of the structural remains. John met Arthur on site the following evening to have a look at what had been found and retrieved a small sample from one of the wood posts for radiocarbon dating.

Figure 27: Arthur at the Sinah Circle site (outlined), Langstone Harbour

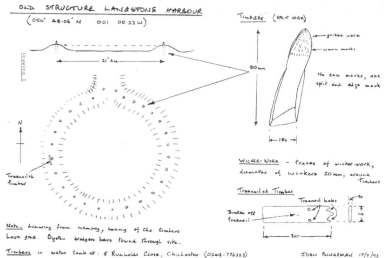

Figure 28: John Bingeman's survey notes – Sinah Circle Structure

A second and more comprehensive investigation of the Sinah Circle, as it came to be known, was undertaken by Hampshire & Wight Trust for Maritime Archaeology (HWTMA; now known as Maritime Archaeology Trust) in July 1993 in which detailed measurements of the timbers were recorded. HWTMA requested protection of the site due to evidence of active erosion, and Langstone Harbour Board subsequently approved a Preservation Order to safeguard the site which was marked with buoys to prevent it from being damaged by trawling or dredging.

The detailed investigation led to an assessment of Sinah Circle's construction being roundwood and split oak timbers, driven stakes, and wattlework – an interwoven lattice of branches and twigs – placed to form an improvised partition or wall. Radiocarbon dating of some of the timbers dated to AD 800-1,000, while other samples tested were returned as being inconclusive. There is also evidence of repair or reuse of the timbers suggesting ongoing maintenance, reconstruction and perhaps even repurposing throughout its history. What this structure was and the function it performed is not definitively known. The placement of the timbers suggested it perhaps had once been a Bronze Age roundhouse dwelling, as it retains similarity to other like-dated structures found on the Isle of

Wight and discovery of Bronze Age worked timber on neighbouring Hayling Island. However, it is conceivable it may rather be an ancient pen for oyster gathering or some other type structure for fishing, which are thought to have been activities practiced in Langstone Harbour for thousands of years. It is also conceivable that the structure had been reused and repaired over many years, explaining the variance of carbon dating results.[10]

Saxon Log Boat

In March of 2002 Arthur was out guiding John Cross from the National Oceanography Centre – University of Southampton around Langstone Harbour, sleuthing the intertidal zone for prehistoric worked flint tools. As they walked the mud flats off the west coast of Long Island in the north area of the harbour, John noticed what appeared to be a partially submerged piece of wood jutting out of the surface – it looked out of place. Arthur came over for a closer look and with his ever-keen eyes noticed adze marks on the surface of the wood (an adze is a tool similar to an axe, with an arched blade at right angles to the handle; used for cutting or shaping large pieces of wood) and knew it was something of significance. The pair contacted HWTMA to alert professional archaeologists to their discovery.

Arrangements were made for an initial inspection to ascertain the context of the find, and then a preliminary survey and recording of the site and artefact later in the month. Upon examination it was determined to be the partial remains of a Dugout – a type of handmade boat fashioned from a hollowed log.

Arthur recalls that one day during the initial investigations, archaeologist Valerie Fenwick with The Nautical Archaeology Society and Sarah Quail with the Portsmouth Public Records Office had come out to review the site. Unfortunately for the pair at one point they found themselves stuck fast in the mud, and Arthur came to their rescue by digging them out.

Owing to the sensitivity of the area and its ecosystem and the need to respect government environmental regulations, a substantive review was deferred until August 2002. In the meantime, the find had garnered considerable media attention with on-site reporting occurring that summer. Arthur and John found themselves in interviews that put both men in the national spotlight and they appeared on a number of programmes including *Southern Ways* on BBC South Today, *Talking Landscapes* on TV6 for BBC2, and *Past Finders* – Topical TV on Meridian.[11]

Figure 29: The Saxon log boat in-situ

The comprehensive fieldwork that followed included topographical survey, soil augering, and analysis of sedimentary layers in and around the location of the log boat. Radiocarbon dating technique applied to a small sample of the wood established the log boat to have been constructed in the early Saxon period at some time in between AD 400-640. The log boat is holed which may suggest it had been damaged whilst in use, and thus offer an explanation as to why it had been abandoned near what at the time was a shallow water channel . It is thought to likely have been used by local inhabitants who lived and foraged for food within the intertidal zone of Langstone Harbour, traveling short distances as part of their foraging routine. According to Julie Satchell, at that time the Head of Research at HWTMA:

The boat and the material found around it provide important information from the early Saxon period, for which little other evidence survives. Research

71

has shown the boat was pulled up onto an area of salt marsh, worked wood pieces trapped under the boat show this area was being used by the local population – possibly for marsh grazing, fowling, or fishing related activity.[12]

Despite the significance of the find, the log boat remained in-situ until the following year. Removal off site, interim storage in a carefully controlled and monitored environment, and subsequent treatment for conservation required funding that was not available to the project. The site was protected from ongoing erosion and environmental exposure with sandbags filled with intertidal mud, and a purpose-built timber structure. Arthur returned to the site regularly to monitor the protective measures that were put in place. Fortunately, the safeguards withstood winter storms that are characteristic of this area and the prehistoric relic was no worse for wear more than a year after its discovery.

In 2003 John and Jane Bingeman, having taken considerable interest in this historically significant find, graciously donated the money needed for the artefact's excavation and recovery by HWTMA. Arthur borrowed John Male's boat and John Bingeman skippered *Wishbone* to transport the HWTMA team out to the site for the recovery. With Arthur's assistance the log boat was carefully removed and transported to the British Ocean Sediment Core Research Facility (BOSCORF) at Southampton Oceanography Centre where it was temporarily housed in a cold storage unit prior to commencement of the next phase of the project – conservation.

The Mary Rose Trust was tasked with conserving the remains of this hollowed-out oak tree log boat, a methodical and painstaking effort of treatment with polyethylene glycol (PEG) and a freeze-drying process, which took seven years to complete. Upon completion it went on display in Portsmouth Museum in 2011. Jennifer Macey, then assistant curator at Portsmouth Museum and Records Service, stated:

Although we know there were small settlements at Buckland and Fratton by the time of the Domesday survey, very little Saxon archaeology has been found in Portsmouth. The log boat will therefore help us to gain a greater understanding of the activities of people in the local area before they settled on Portsea Island.[13]

Several other archaeological finds came about as a result of Arthur and John Cross's investigations including the discovery of other artefacts and human-built structures in the vicinity of the log boat. The finds included other timber post and wattlework structures radiocarbon dated to AD 790-1,030, hearths, numerous examples of worked flint pieces and pottery fragments, and a significant deposit of burnt flint hypothesised to be a Bronze Age burnt mound – a site where steam was created by dropping fire-heated stone into water – possibly for bathing, cooking, or other purposes.[14] On the assumption that the log boat and other artefacts had remained undisturbed throughout history, the sedimentary layers that preserved these artefacts for thousands of years were studied to shed light on past climate, sea levels and daily life in the south of England.

The significant find of the log boat, in part to Arthur's credit, was only the second of its kind found in the Solent since the 1880s.[15]

Figure 30: Saxon log boat on display in Portsmouth Museum

Funerary Urn

Figure 31: Arthur examining a burial urn in-situ

One day in late November 2002 Arthur and John Bingeman were traversing the foreshore of Long Island when Arthur spotted a faint circular outline projecting slightly from the saturated mud surface. A return visit and examination identified it to be a Bronze Age urn. The site was surveyed, and GPS coordinates established to document the find. In the following month Arthur returned to monitor site conditions and found it to be in jeopardy due to its exposure to the environment. John determined that it had to be removed before it was lost to the tides, and the pair performed what could be considered an emergency excavation.

The urn and its contents were found to be completely waterlogged and the top rim of the pottery was partly compromised due to erosive action of water and sediment load. Despite these circumstances the find was significant as the urn contents had remained intact and were confirmed as human bone fragments and teeth – established to be those of an adult female and a child.

The conserved urn and its contents are presently held in the collections of Portsmouth Museum. During Arthur's exploits in Langstone Harbour he has discovered a total of ten burial urns.

Wealdon Stone Face

Arthur would often sleuth around the north islands of Langstone Harbour on his own, and in December of 2002 he was investigating stratified sedimentary layers of the soil ledges found on the west edge of Long Island. He happened upon a partially exposed rock measuring some 4.7 inches in height by 2.8 inches across, amidst concentrations of prehistoric pottery sherds, charcoal and burnt flint, and bone fragments. This however was no ordinary rock as on one side appeared the likeness of a human face with a defined mouth, nose, eyes, and brow. Arthur photographed the rock in-situ and then removed it for subsequent research.

The specimen was soon identified as Wealdon sandstone which is a classic sedimentary rock common to southern England. The origin of what is likened to that of a human face has been debated amongst professionals and academics alike: On one hand it has been suggested that the facial likeness is merely coincidental and is the result of the natural fracturing patterns in the rock. However, late Professor David Peacock of the University of Southampton and Professor Richard Bradley with the University of Reading, both considered subject experts in their fields of study, examined the piece and concluded it had been formed with tools and thus was of human origin. It has also been suggested the piece could represent Neanderthal art, and it may be up to 24,000 years old. A similar carved stone head was found in a cave in northern France and dates to approximately 28,000 BC; at this time in history Britain was still connected to mainland Europe before sea level rose to create the English Channel.

Figure 32: Wealdon Stone Face

Although the find was amongst a field of Bronze Age artefacts, the historical timeline which the piece belongs to remains undefined. Arthur believes that because of the proximity of the stone head find to a documented Middle to Late Bronze Age funerary urn field, there may be an association of the artefact to burials and perhaps it is an effigy or a commemoration of a deceased individual. The Wealdon Stone Face is on display in Portsmouth Museum.

Part IV

Anecdotes from Arthur's Life

Luck or Fate?

Anyone who has come to know Arthur well is familiar with his uncanny ability to uncover historical finds and treasures. Whereas anyone else might walk past some object of significance hidden buried in the ground, Arthur being in the same location will home-in on some clue or triviality to make the find. There are many compelling instances such that one cannot help but question there being some transcendence or act of nature that blesses Arthur with this gift. The following events from Arthur's life are but a mere sampling and are included with other colourful stories from his life for posterity.

Chance Finds

Four yarns in Arthur's own words

One day in 1971 whilst bait digging for ragworm in Langstone harbour, I was working my way across the mud flats when I saw a short length of old rusty chain showing through the mud. I walked over to it and pulled hard – it was attached to a large concrete mooring block. From experience I knew that the worms tend to live around such obstructions under the mud and so I started digging around the old block.

It is worth noting that I used a flat-pronged potato fork. The broad prongs help turn the soft mud over. This also means that any small objects with holes in them would not slide up and snag on the prongs. You can imagine my surprise when after a couple of forkfuls of mud, there stuck right on the point at the end of one of the prongs was a gold ring! It was in the form of a coiled snake starting with the tail and ending with the head wrapping across the coils. On the overlap were several diamonds.

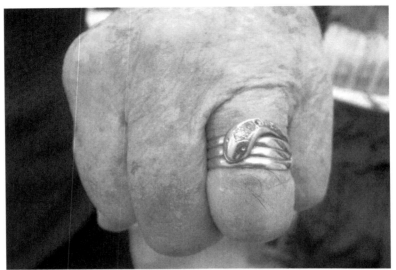

Figure 33: Arthur's snake ring found in Portsmouth Harbour

I pocketed my find and later on in a moment of free time I took it to H Samuel Jewellers. They examined it and confirmed it was 18 karat gold and Victorian Age in origin and set in it were rose-cut diamonds. They estimated it to be in the region of 100 years old. The ring fit my hand perfectly and I still wear it to this very day.

***

Whilst on holiday some years ago in Cornwall, Gina and I were enjoying a walk down an old pathway leading down to the coastline and sea pool near Bude. Halfway down the path, something glinted in the sunlight which caught my eye. I bent down to see what it was and there in front of me half-covered by the soft white sand was a gold earring. I picked it up and showed it to Gina who commented 'you and your luck again'. It went straight into my pocket. A little further along the path we saw a couple of young ladies walking towards us who were clearly looking for something on the ground. As we approached them, I asked 'what are you looking for?' One of them, who was almost in tears, said

'I have lost one of my gold earrings given to me by my mother'

I reached into my pocket and with a grin on my face I pulled out the earring and replied to her 'do you mean this one?'

She was delighted to be reunited with the keepsake but astonished that I had found such a small object in the sandy shrub-laden ground that made up the pathway.

***

During the time of finding all the wonderful artefacts on the Invincible, Gina & I together with her brother Tom and sister-in-law Gwen, went to France to get away from it all for a short while. We stayed in the Loire Valley and during our time there visited the beautiful and historic (built in 1404) Château de La Barre. Walking through the wonderful gardens of the Château we noticed a pile of shingle and rubbish where some workers had been clearing the stream that ran through the gardens. All the debris had been piled up on the bank alongside the stream. Such was my curiosity that we ambled over to have a look. As we reached the spoil heap, I noticed a small shape that appeared to be out of place at the top of the pile. I clambered up and found it to be an old, silver plated medallion of some sort.

After rubbing the dirt from it, based on the decoration stamped into the face of it, I immediately realised it was very old and kept it to check it later. It may date back as far as the 18th century. I still have the medallion in the collection of things I've come across over the years.

Figure 34: The medallion found by Arthur
***

On one of my many days of fishing in the 1970s I was down in Portsmouth Harbour to fish for bass off one of the pontoons at the edge of the Dockyard. I firstly had to dig some ragworm to bait my line. On that day, for some reason I went to the exact same spot as I used to 'mudlark' to earn my keep

83

as a youngster. Just as I did back in those days, I followed the edge of the old jetty from where the holiday makers threw money into the mud. I started digging for the ragworm when I came across a couple of old pennies – this made me smile, thinking – 'just like the old days'. Clearly, they were pennies that us old mudlarks had missed. After a short while I turned over a pile of mud but instead of ragworms there was a small perfectly round ring showing through the black ooze of the Harbour's ancient mud. After cleaning it I found it was gold which was later identified as 14 karat. It had a St Christopher on the face. St Christopher, the patron saint of travellers. Even now, I sometimes wonder if the ring was lost by someone back in the era of mud-larking who was walking along the old walkway to catch a boat to go travelling somewhere. I can just imagine someone throwing a couple of pennies over to watch us lot getting filthy while racing each other to grab the money, and perhaps the act of throwing the pennies caused the ring to fly off his finger? Someone else's misfortune was my good luck.

Figure 35: St Christopher ring from the mud of The Hard

Lost and Found – 'An Absolutely True Story'

By John Broomhead

On the 14th of June 1986, John Bingeman was out with the team in his boat *Viney Peglar*, excavating on the *Invincible* wreck when he uncovered a small fishing frame. You know the type, just like the ones you can buy when on holiday to go crabbing or fishing off the end of a pier. It was just a simple frame made up of four pieces of wood joined at the corners. In antiquity it would have had some type of fishing line or cord wound around two of the frame pieces opposite each other.

He found this delightful little personal object from where it had laid buried and undisturbed in the seabed sediment for more than 220 years. The nails joining the four pieces together had all corroded away over the centuries on the seabed and so the pieces of wood, although still in situ on the wreck, were nevertheless four separate items. John put the pieces of the frame into his dry suit pocket and after finishing his dive returned to the surface and the dive boat.

John said with a happy note in his voice *'Look Arthur, I have found you a fishing square'*.

He reached into his pocket but there were only three out of the four pieces inside! He then said in a less happy voice *'Oh blast, I have lost one of the pieces'*.

Bear in mind that the wreck lies three miles offshore and the tidal flow is very strong at times and despite all the precautions taken, just occasionally items get swept away on a journey into the depths of the channel.

The small piece of wood approximately 6 inches long by 5/8 inches wide by 5/16 inches thick, representing just the tiniest of a speck in the ocean it was, after centuries lying together on the wreck now departed from the other pieces. We accepted that it was sadly lost forever. Or was it?

Several months later in October of the same year, Arthur was walking along Southsea beach in the aftermath of some stormy weather. The sea was still running quite high with a heavy swell and there was a huge amount of weed and debris being washed up along the tide line. Suddenly, in amongst all the weed and flotsam that a wave had just deposited on the shoreline, something caught Arthur's eye. Now remember that he was a fisherman, and as such relied to some degree on his luck. That little something that had caught his eye was a small piece of wood and appeared to be the same size and colour as the other three parts of the fishing frame that had been recovered back in the summer. He picked it up and took it back to the project's Conservation Laboratory and guess what – the original nail holes and corrosion stains lined up exactly with the other pieces. Arthur had found the missing piece.

Consider that this missing piece had been washing around the fast-flowing tidal waters of the Solent and edge of the English Channel for about three months! Was this just luck or was it a higher authority that saw fit to put Arthur on that precise spot at that precise time when that tiny speck in the ocean washed up at his feet?

Having been directly and intimately involved in the project from the outset and knowing all the other very strange things that happened during the excavation years, I personally find it all rather spooky.

Soon after this happened a local radio station, BBC Radio Solent, started a programme called *The Late Show* with Nick Girdler. In one of his programmes Nick would tell his listeners short, spooky anecdotes of things that had happened to him such as putting an object down somewhere and then soon afterwards going to get it, only to find it was no longer where he had put it and unable to locate it after an extensive search. Then, the following day, the item turns up in a place that he absolutely knew he had already searched.

He asked listeners who had experienced similar events to call in and he would read out their stories. Of course, I wrote in with the tale of the missing object that found its way to Arthur who reunited it with the other parts it had belonged to, in its seabed resting place for the past two hundred years. In this instance the owner did not find the missing object, but rather the object found the owner!

Witness to International Espionage

On 18th April 1956 Arthur had gone out night-fishing for sea bass and pollock from the Gosport Ferry Pontoon on the Portsmouth side of the Harbour. It was midweek and Arthur had settled into a quiet evening. Across the water some 200 yards to the northwest, the Soviet Cruiser *Ordzhonikidze* was moored alongside the South Railway Jetty located in the southwest periphery of the Naval Base. The ship had arrived earlier that day, carrying Soviet Communist Party leader Nikita Khrushchev on a 10-day diplomatic visit to meet with Prime Minister Anthony Eden. In the aura of mistrust that existed between the Cold War adversaries, the Soviet Naval Spetsnaz – a specialised military unit of commando frogmen – was tasked with conducting underwater patrols around the vessels whilst docked at Portsmouth.

Figure 36: Arrival of the *Ordzhonikidze* in Portsmouth Harbour

Arthur remembers how the evening calm was interrupted by powerful arc spotlights on the *Ordzhonikidze* being lit up and trained on the waters around the ship, soon followed by commotion both on the vessel and alongside on the jetty; this went on for about an hour as Arthur looked on in surprise and curiosity. At the time it was obvious to Arthur that something significant had occurred.

He learned afterward that he had been witness to an event that became a politically charged espionage mystery which captured the attention of the world and would be known to history as the 'Crabb Affair'.[16,17]

As the story goes, former Royal Navy Lieutenant Commander and naval frogman Lionel 'Buster' Crabb had been brought out of retirement by MI6 – the British Secret Intelligence Service. His mission was to investigate the hull of the *Ordzhonikidze* as the ship was regarded to be very agile in service, and the Navy was keen to become acquainted with her design. Crabb had undertaken a similar mission the year prior and so he was the most suited candidate.

Arthur recalls that the *Ordzhonikidze's* impressive manoeuvrability was attributed to its propellers and side thrusters built into its hull. Crabb's mission was to enter the water, approach the ship and perform underwater reconnaissance without being detected.

Two days before the mission Crabb and an MI6 Operative named Matthew Smith checked in at the Sally Port Inn on Hight Street, close to the mouth of Portsmouth Harbour.

The official account, as published, is that Crabb and Smith left the hotel well before dawn on 19th April and walked to the Dockyard where they were met by a Navy Officer from the Base, the Senior Clearance Diver with *HMS Vernon*, and the local Chief Detective Superintendent acting in the capacity of police liaison. They boarded *HMS Maidstone*, docked at the South Camber which was only 70 metres from where the *Ordzhonikidze* was moored, and Crabb was readied for his dive. He apparently entered the water shortly before 07.00 and was spotted by Russian sailors nearly an hour later from the sterns of the accompanying Destroyers. It is hypothesised that Crabb had encountered difficulty during his dive, perhaps due to the fact he was not in good physical shape and may have experienced oxygen or carbon dioxide toxicity and was forced to surface. The story follows that a search was initiated at 09.15 by navy men aboard the launch of the *Maidstone*, and then a subsequent search soon afterward.

Figure 37: Lieutenant Lionel 'Buster' Crabb, RNVR

Later that morning the MI6 operative checked both himself and the absent Commander Crabb out of the hotel with both men's luggage in hand, paid cash and left. Two days later, Police Chief Detective Superintendent Lamport visited the hotel, tore out the pages of the hotel's register which documented the men's stay and threatened the Sally Port Inn's owner that if he did not cooperate or spoke of the event in any way, he would be charged under the Official Secrets Act. On 29th April, the Admiralty issued an internal memorandum advising that any media inquiry regarding Commander Crabb's disappearance should be answered that he had been declared missing and presumed dead due to an accident having occurred whilst testing experimental diving gear. This supposedly occurred in Stokes Bay which is a few miles to the west of Portsmouth. It is thought that the Prime Minister's Office was desperate to keep the story out of the media while the Russian envoy was on his diplomatic visit and his ships were still in Portsmouth Harbour.

The following day the media broke the news story speculating that Lionel Crabb was missing and had been caught trying to spy on the foreign warships at Portsmouth, was incarcerated and taken back to the Soviet Union. On 4th May the Russians issued a public communiqué to the British government advising that the visiting ships' crews had witnessed a British diver approaching the ships, and they demanded an explanation. The government's reply was that

> *The Frogman, who was reported in the Soviet note, was discovered from the Soviet ships swimming between the Soviet Destroyers, was to all appearances Commander Crabb. His presence in the vicinity of the Destroyers occurred without any permission whatever, and Her Majesty's Government express their regret for this incident.*

At this point Lionel Crabb's body was still unaccounted for. The mystery deepened when more than a year later, on 9th June 1957, the headless and handless decomposed corpse of a middle-aged man in navy dive gear was found by fishermen in Chichester Harbour, east of Portsmouth eleven miles down the coast. While the body was assumed to be that of Crabb, autopsy results were inconclusive, and worse yet there were inferences of report tampering. Identification was further complicated in the possibility that the body was that of another diver, perhaps even one related to the same incident.

As one may imagine, various explanations and conspiracy theories abound as to what had occurred. In 2006, archival information was released under the Freedom of Information Act; there was evidence that Crabb had a diving partner on his fateful assignment. Other British and Russian records have since been sealed and will not be opened until 2057 – clearly there remains a will to keep the truth secret for what must be significant reasons. In

2007 former Spetsnaz commando diver Eduard Koltsov, who had participated in the 1956 state visit to Portsmouth, was interviewed by the BBC. He stated that he had encountered Crabb beneath the *Ordzhonikidze* and a struggle ensued in which he slit the man's throat. In that interview he displayed the knife he claims to have used, and the Order of the Red Star awarded to him for his actions.

What is acknowledged today is there has been a massive cover-up by both the governments involved in the Crabb Affair, and the truth has been withheld from the public at large. Factual inconsistencies abound, and the official explanation seems both unreasonable and unbelievable. For example, if at the time there was so much risk in the exposure of the failed spy mission damaging the diplomatic relations associated with Khrushchev's visit, why were search parties supposedly sent out in broad daylight on the morning of the occurrence? Surely it makes more sense that MI6 would have abandoned Crabb simply to maintain plausible deniability. At the heart of such unanswered questions is the fact that Arthur had seen a significant incident occur the night before; plenty of things could have transpired or outcomes plotted in that time gap. Perhaps Arthur's observations will one day be explained by factual documentation that is eventually declassified by the government.

Close Call

As recalled by Arthur Mack and John M. Bingeman

On 19th May 1987, the project team was out on the *Invincible* wreck site. Arthur was working on the dive boat, attending to the needs of the crew as he so often did – helping divers in and out of their gear, operating the air compressor for the airlift, refilling breathing gas cylinders, and the like. Michael Smith, a Naval Petty Officer on the excavation team, was working the *Invincible* site that day. He left the wreck and travelled along the seabed in search of lobsters and was some 50 yards to the north of the ship when he encountered a large cylindrical object some 6 feet in length and 26 inches in diameter. While examining it he scratched its surface with his diver's knife, investigating a hunch that perhaps it was made of an alloy metal. He surfaced to inform John Bingeman who had responsibility for the dive and excavation operations. John himself a Royal Navy Officer familiar with munitions realised the significance of what the diver had encountered.

The work stopped abruptly, and a call was immediately placed to *HMS Vernon* Bomb Disposal Team to send divers in for investigation. The object was confirmed to be a WWII era German 'Luftmine Type A' parachute mine armed with an 1100-pound (500 kilogram) Hexanite explosive charge, also known by its American designation 'GC2' and in the United Kingdom by the Admiralty as 'Type D'.[18] The *Luftwaffe* dropped a recorded 38 parachute mines on Portsmouth city alone between July 1940 and July 1944, though many more likely went unrecorded.[19] These devices could cause considerable damage by imparting a deadly shockwave. Used as a sea mine, a single unit could disable and sink a vessel on or under the water, and as a land mine could destroy multiple homes or other buildings.

According to the Imperial War Museum[20]

There were two types of magnetic sea mines used by the Germans, who termed them the Luftmine A (LMA) of 500kg, and the Luftmine B (LMB) of 1000kg. The Luftwaffe began dropping magnetic mines into the waters around Britain during November 1939, first from He115 and He111 aircraft. The mines were cylindrical in shape with a hemispherical nose and deployed under a 27ft diameter green artificial silk parachute, falling at about 40mph. They were fitted with magnetic firing and later with acoustic or magnetic/acoustic firing.

When the mine hit the water and sank to more than 8 feet depth, hydrostatic pressure and the dissolution of a soluble plug actuated the magnetic device and the mine became operational against shipping. The mine was also armed with a clockwork bomb fuze which caused the bomb to explode when used against land targets, and this was started by the impact of hitting the ground. The mine was timed to detonate 25 seconds after the fuze had started. When deployed at sea, the time fuze did not operate as a diaphragm stopped the clockwork when under the pressure of 7 feet of water or more. The first intentional use of magnetic mines against land targets was on the night of 16 September 1940, when the mines with their charge/weight ratio of 60-70% explosive caused considerable blast damage in built up areas. Inevitably, they became known to the British populace as Land Mines.

The following week, *HMS Vernon* Bomb Disposal Team removed the mine from the seabed and then towed it out further offshore. With Portsmouth and Langstone Harbours closed to boat traffic, the World War II artefact was exploded.

The centuries-old remains of the *Invincible* had escaped modern damage and perhaps even destruction, as fortunately the mine had not been dropped closer to the wreck site – notwithstanding the fact it did not detonate during the war nor anytime afterward. The ship, its artefacts, the acquired knowledge, and contribution to history attributable to its discovery, may have suffered irreparably.

Submerged Surprise

By John Broomhead

During the early days of the project, after finding what at the time was an unknown wreck, Arthur and myself became totally absorbed by the maritime archaeological bug. Arthur had learned to dive and made his first open water dive to the wreck on 13th June 1981. Looking back, that first dive did not gain us any brownie points on the health & safety front! There were just the two of us in *Wishbone* and after I initially dived to clear the weed, back aboard *Wishbone* Arthur readied himself for the dive. Although he had completed some pool training, you will understand that he was a little nervous about going into the depths where there were no sides of a pool, and after a few metres down there would also be neither surface nor bottom to see – just a vast emptiness. Now the safety part, we both entered the water leaving *Wishbone* anchored to the seabed, and although there was a diving 'A' flag up there was no one acting as surface cover. Just a small empty boat bobbing on the sea three miles offshore.

After several dives on *Invincible* he had gained so much confidence that I asked him if he fancied diving on the *Impregnable* (1799) wreck site and he eagerly said yes. Once again, off we went, just the two of us in *Wishbone*. The wreck lies relatively close inshore and so our positional landmarks stood out making it a simple job to locate the wreck. We towed a small grapple along and that 'always exciting' moment came when the towing warp tightened, and *Wishbone* came to an abrupt halt.

We put our diving kit on and raised the diving 'A' flag, warning boats to keep clear: *'Divers in the water'*. We slipped over the side and into the shallow water, only 4 to 5 metres depth, and were soon on the wreck. As we slowly worked along the wreckage, I could see that

Arthur's breathing was calm and easy – a sure sign he was relaxed and enjoying himself. The first thing that caught Arthur's eye were the large cast iron ballast blocks piled high on the remains of the keel and heavily corroded together after 180 years on the seabed. Next, we found a pile of 32lb shot (cannon balls) and further along, the shiny copper keel bolts still firmly fixed into the keel, came into view. I say shiny because being copper they were not encrusted with marine life but were being kept polished by tidal action. We both tried to find Broad Arrow marks but there were none to be found.

Perhaps I shouldn't have done so, but I left Arthur checking the copper keel bolts and dropped down to the seabed, to see if I could find a lobster for my dinner in one of the many holes beneath the old timbers. I found a creature of interest but before disturbing it, I went back to find Arthur. Using hand signals, I gestured that he should follow me. I put my head close to the hole and then slowly came away and indicated for Arthur to do the same and look inside. The hole was dark and in order to see anything, the method is to put your head up close to the entrance of the hole to block out the ambient light. Your eyes then become accustomed to the dark and whatever is inside starts to come into focus.

As Arthur did this, he suddenly took a very quick intake of breath, resulting in him increasing his buoyancy and so he shot up to the surface in what divers term a runaway ascent. The water was only shallow and so no harm done but I followed him up to make sure he was OK. He swore at me – again – and we called an end to diving. So, what had he seen? It certainly was not a lobster in the hole. Once Arthur's eyes had become acclimated and in focus to the inside of the hole, looking back at him were a pair of large grey rubbery lips and two big shiny, beady eyes. It was a rather large conger eel.

Back aboard *Wishbone* Arthur saw the funny side – eventually.

The Return to *Invincible*

By Brent Piniuta

10.30 in the morning of Sunday, 1st May 2016 found me standing up against the stern of a small fishing boat named *Nicole* that was pitching from side to side with the waves on the water. Standing right in front of me was an older gentleman whom I had met not thirty minutes earlier, and now he was gesturing me to get off the boat.

I was apprehensive to dive in unfamiliar waters but had spent the last two years preparing for that moment and would have instant regret if I backed out. I leaned over the transom of the boat and dropped into the water, rechecked my gear, and made my way along the swim line rigged outboard of the starboard side of *Nicole*. I followed it up to the bow where it was hooked to the anchor cable which angled downward, disappearing beyond in the direction of the seabed. That was my experience meeting Arthur Mack, and it will be burned into my memory for the rest of my life.

This story begins some six years earlier in 2010 when I came upon John Broomhead's story of finding the remains of the *Invincible* and the team's effort to excavate the shipwreck. In September of 2012 I visited John who lives on Hayling Island, across Langstone Harbour from Eastney.

A short walk from his home found us on the south beach of Hayling Island, where he pointed out to me the location of the *Invincible* wreck which lay halfway between there and the northeast shores of the Isle of Wight. In light-hearted jest he said I should hire dive gear and go out to see the wreck for myself. As tempting as his suggestion was, I recall laughing in reply because not only did I have no scuba training, I held a lifelong aversion to stepping into water 'where living things lurk'.

Figure 38: Arthur at the stern of *Nicole* and Melvin Gofton at the helm

About a year later the Nautical Archaeology Society (NAS) which is based out of Fort Cumberland on Portsea Island, advertised an opportunity to join a group dive on the *Invincible* wreck, as part of NAS's educational programme. The *Invincible's* Protected Wreck designation remains to this day, and so generally only archaeologists and those of similar status enjoy the privilege of diving the site. I contacted John and told him that if I could obtain the diving qualifications, I would make the trip back to dive on the wreck and asked if he would care to join me? At age 65, John had not dived on the wreck in nearly 25 years but still had a lingering desire *'to see the old girl'* once more.

Two summers of scuba training later, my diving certifications were in place and in May 2016 I crossed the Atlantic once again. Upon arrival I learned that transportation arrangements to the wreck site had been made through Arthur Mack who had a friend with a boat that had been hired for our excursion. The anticipation of the dive was on my mind, but I was excited for the chance to finally meet Arthur, the man I came to admire for finding the *Invincible* and launching the fascinating story that ensued. On the day of our dive we awoke to a sunny, calm morning which was a relief. In the weeks leading up to the event John warned me there had been rough, stormy weather on the south coast, and worse yet it had churned up the seabed to make for poor underwater visibility. John and I drove out to the Eastney-Hayling Ferry Terminal at the southwest tip of Hayling Island. We dropped our gear at the end of the pontoon and John, looking into deep water alongside, remarked how incredibly crystal clear it was, which was a complete reversal of conditions from only days earlier – *'the diving gods were smiling down on us'* I recall one of us quipped. Moments later he pointed out a small fishing vessel approaching the terminal as it crossed the inlet of Langstone Harbour, saying it must be *'them'*. I rushed off to park the car on land and hurry back across the pontoon, as by that time John was aboard and everyone was waiting on me.

Stepping onto the boat was a bit overwhelming. All but a stranger to me, Arthur Mack shook my hand with a firm grip and greeted me aboard with a great big smile. There was really no questioning who among the men Arthur was as he had the physical stance and frame of a strong man – someone who had spent the better part of his life tending to nets and trawls. And he was wearing a black Fiddler cap, which by my accounts from having seen pictures of him in books, was practically his 'trademark'.

It was rather surreal to be crowded in on this small boat with the men who had undertaken the *Invincible* Project some thirty years before. Not only that, but the skipper and owner of our boat *Nicole* was Melvin Gofton. Almost 37 years to the day Arthur had been out with Melvin in his boat *Vanessa* when their fishing net snagged *Invincible's* timbers. It really felt as though I had taken a step back in time.

As we left the harbour and headed due south into the Solent, I listened to the men reminisce over the times they shared making that very trip before. The conversation was light and humorous, marked with laughter over the din of *Nicole's* engine which advanced us closer to the wreck. It was enjoyable listening but a distraction from the task at hand – getting into our dive gear. The boat was equipped with GPS to locate us on the wreck coordinates, yet I noticed Arthur and John Bingeman taking visual transits with landmarks to the north and No Man's Land and Horse Sand Forts to the west of our position, as they had done so many times in the past.

Figure 39: Looking back at *Nicole* before descending on the wreck

Arriving at the wreck site, the boat's anchor was set and one by one we entered the water. Arthur was reliving his duties as divemaster throughout the excavation work of the 1980s, assisting with our gear and helping us off the boat. I held John Bingeman in the highest regard, and still do, for diving with us at the age of 82 as most divers would have retired their dive gear many years before. Scuba gear for cold water diving is heavy, cumbersome, and restrictive, and so core strength and stamina are requirements of the activity. John Bingeman disappeared below to meet up with the government-appointed licensee who has care and control of the *Invincible* wreck site and oversaw our visit. John Broomhead took his turn, and just as he left the swim line I went in next.

Passing through green nothingness to a depth of 26 feet, I arrived on the seabed. John had stopped at the end of the anchor line, looking back, and awaiting my arrival since our plan was to pair up for the dive. Just off to my left was John Bingeman, tending to his equipment. I paused to orient myself to our location on the wreck and then looked over my camera equipment to ensure all was in order.

Figure 40: Arriving at the seabed

Following behind John we traversed a reel line that was set out for us across the site, so that we could find our way around and then back. The recent storms had shifted sand to expose even more of the wreck. Not only did we have a fine view of the 'skeleton' of the ship – massive timber frames which were of a scale and size I could not have imagined, but newly revealed artefacts dotted the inner port side of the hull: a coil of rope, a barrel head, numerous lead scuppers, and other features all around us. Indeed, on that dive two loose and at-risk artefacts were retrieved from the seabed by the licensee, lest they otherwise be lost to the tide or decay – a leather shoe once owned by one of *Invincible's* crewmen, and a double-pulley rigging block. The end of the reel line found us at a large section of the lower starboard side of the hull, which at some point in history had broken off from the rest of the ship. It was an impressive but poignant sight, recognizing how this once-magnificent ship had come to a sad end.

Our dive on the *Invincible*, albeit short at only 35 minutes, was a success and back on deck there were smiles all round as we shed our gear for warm clothes, chatted about what we had seen on the wreck, and took pictures to mark a memorable day.

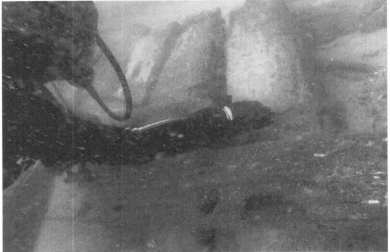

Figure 41: John Broomhead examining *Invincible's* timbers

After returning our dive gear later that afternoon we stopped in at Arthur and Gina's home in Eastney for a visit. I learned that while the 'Original 3' team of Arthur, John and John had not been together for several years, it had also been decades since the trio had been back on the wreck as the project team. So while the plan had simply been to dive the *Invincible*, a reunion amongst old friends had taken place. For me it was and remains an honour to have been a part of, knowing it may never take place in that special way again.

Figure 42: John Bingeman & Arthur with an *Invincible* artefact

Figure 43: The 'Original 3' – John Bingeman, Arthur & John Broomhead

Thomas Shepherd – Connection to the Past?

By Brent Piniuta

After the adventure of diving the wreck of the *Invincible*, I awaited the next opportunity to return to England. It was later that year a major announcement was made: Significant funding had been earmarked to launch a four-year project to continue excavations on the *Invincible* wreck site, to rescue at-risk artefacts being exposed by changing seabed conditions. The end of the excavation and conservation programme would be marked with a new exhibition launched by the National Museum of the Royal Navy in conjunction with Chatham Historic Dockyard Trust to share *Invincible's* story with the world.

In May 2018 I returned to England with a number of activities on my 'must-do' list. One of the highlights was a long time coming – Visiting The National Archives at Kew to pursue research regarding the crew assembled on the *Invincible*, and workers in Portsmouth Dockyard who had readied the ship for the second expedition to Louisbourg in early 1758. Historical documents of interest were photographed with a plan to conduct research upon returning home.

I also spent time in the Portsmouth area and had the opportunity to visit Arthur and Gina. I cannot adequately share with you the charm of listening to Arthur tell stories of his past archaeological exploits, and to see the sparkle in his eyes which shows the passion he has in his soul for history. Arthur shared with me an interesting story from Gina's family heritage: The Shepherd family has deep roots in Portsmouth and a longstanding association with the Dockyard and the Royal Navy in general. The family's tradition has been that the first-born son of each generation was named Thomas, and when old enough continued the family tradition of working in the employ of Portsmouth Dockyard.

Arthur asked if I could investigate the prospect of a Thomas Shepherd working in the Dockyard during the time of *Invincible*. He had read in literature that Thomas Slade – Surveyor of the Navy circa 1755, had met a Shipwright *'Thomas Shepperd – a very good man'* during his visit to Portsmouth Dockyard on 9th October 1756, which incidentally preceded Arthur's Birthday by exactly 178 years. While fascinated with the story of Gina's family tradition, I also believed in it – because of the luck or fate seemingly connected with Arthur's existence.

Upon returning home from the trip I began combing through the hundreds of document images taken at The National Archives, of what are called Pay Books for Portsmouth Dockyard – records of employees and their wages paid out in the conduct of business at the Dockyard. You can imagine my surprise that when I came to page 19 of the list of Shipwrights – skilled carpenters that built and repaired ships – that had worked in the Dockyard in 1758, there in plain sight at the top of the ledger was the listing of a Thomas Shepherd. It appeared that he was a Senior Shipwright based on his rate of pay, and he had a servant reporting to him, a Mr James Ring.

Learning this news, Arthur was fascinated of the prospect of a connection. However, a formidable task lay ahead to validate the inference that the Shipwright Thomas Shepherd was one of Gina's ancestors. Historical documentation of births, deaths and marriages are available in the public records domain, but the knowledge and practical experience of a genealogist is necessary to undertake a review.

In the summer of that same year I embarked on a project to document the names of all the crew put aboard *Invincible* for the Louisbourg expedition of 1758. In November I followed up on a tip that the National Museum of the Royal Navy was seeking assistance to undertake historical research that would contribute to the forthcoming museum exhibition, and I joined a team of local Portsmouth volunteers. Upon learning that some of my colleagues had genealogy research expertise, the story of the Shepherd family was passed along to Maxine Higgins who set to task to investigate.

Her research traced the family lineage as far back as 1818. Between that time and the present, the evidence of the Shepherd family tradition was indisputable: Gina's father Thomas Charles Shepherd, born 1912, served in the Royal Navy based out of Portsmouth and retired as a Chief Petty Officer. Born in 1875, Thomas John Shepherd's occupation was listed as 'Boy' serving at HM Gunwharf Portsmouth, at age 16. Thomas (Roy) Reed Shepherd born in 1850 was a Joiner – a type of dockyard carpenter who crafted fittings, deck furniture and ornamentation on ships. There are contemporary records of Thomas Shepherds enlisted in the Royal Navy whom had received the Naval General Service Medal (1793-1840): An Able Seaman who served in the 4th rate 50-gun *Isis* at the Battle of Copenhagen in 1801, and a Royal Marine Private in the 5th rate 36-gun *Pique* off Syria in 1840, though the prospect of family association has not been investigated.

The further back in time one investigates historical records, the more the thread is compromised by the passage of time due to incomplete, lost or destroyed archival documentation. This is the case in the review of the Shepherds, and so perhaps two generations worth of information are needed to unequivocally confirm the relation between Thomas Shepherd of 1758 and Thomas Shepherd born in Portsea in 1818. Nonetheless, given the pattern of family tradition it is reasonable to infer that Arthur's wife Gina may be a descendent of Thomas Shepherd, Shipwright in Portsmouth Dockyard at the time of the *Invincible*.

The connection does not end there. Months after the *Invincible* wrecked on 19th February 1758 and was abandoned days later, the ship eventually was declared a total loss by the Navy Board. Throughout the spring and summer of 1758 work crews were sent out from the Dockyard to salvage as many stores and as much equipment from the ship as possible, given that about only half of the ship was underwater having run aground on a shallow sand bank.

Several years before I had researched circa-1758 British newspapers reporting on the loss of the *Invincible*. One such publication, The Public Advertiser, No. 7413, dated 11 August 1758 included a heading of 'Port News', and from Portsmouth on the 9th of August it stated:

> *Two Gangs of Shipwrights are gone from the Dockyard, to tear down as much of the Upper Works of the Invincible as possible. A Tender* [a transport boat] *lies off, on board of which they lie at Nights, and a large Dock Lighter* [another type of work boat] *is along-side. The Two Gangs are to be relieved every Week by two others, till ordered to leave off.*

This fact opens the door to the possibility that Thomas Shepherd, Shipwright, had been sent out to *Invincible* to assist with her teardown. Given that he was a Senior Shipwright responsible for supervision of subordinates, it is likely he was among the 'Gangs of Shipwrights' sent to work on the *Invincible* in the summer of 1758. Contemplate then, the notion that in 1956 Arthur married Gina Shepherd whose ancestor may have helped dismantle the *Invincible* – the very ship he would go on to discover the remains of in 1979. Would you agree it is beyond coincidence?

Epilogue

As this story started with an account of Arthur's birthplace it seems most fitting to come full circle and end it there. In November 2012 Arthur wrote an editorial letter published in the Portsmouth Evening News, suggesting that as it was the 800th anniversary of Portsmouth's first Royal Dockyard there ought to be some formal acknowledgement such as a Blue Plaque to celebrate its historical significance.

In 1194 King Richard I granted a Royal Charter to Portsmouth, permitting trade with other towns. This was the birth of the future city of Portsmouth, which grew from humble origins as a small fishing hamlet.[21] Richard I also ordered a dock to be built there for his ships which he used for travel between England and his possessions in France. Some eighteen years later King John, Richard's successor and younger brother, was using Portsmouth to embark and disembark from royal expeditions, and in 1212 he ordered that the dockyard be protected with *'a good and strong wall'* to shelter royal ships from winter weather and provide secure harbourage. However, the first naval dock at Portsmouth was in a different location than it is today. A study of archival information by historians and academics revealed that the inlet to the original dock was some 400 yards south east of Victory Gate in present-day St. Georges Square, and the dock and associated buildings extended northward in a location that is now bounded by Victory Road to the west, Butcher Street to the east, and College Lane to the north. It seems rather unnecessary to point out the remarkable fact that Arthur's humble birthplace in College Lane is quite literally the cradle of the country's Navy. Might Arthur's lifelong connection to the sea and his extraordinary maritime finds be attributable to this association in some way?

Arthur turned to John Bingeman to implement his idea of a commemoration for Portsmouth Dockyard's 800th anniversary, knowing that John's association with regional historical and archaeological institutions would be the catalyst for success. After an undertaking of research, networking, facilitation, fundraising, and development, on 26th September 2014 Lord Mayor of Portsmouth Cllr Steven Wylie unveiled an illustrated commemorative board in St. Georges Square. Arthur was pleased to see his idea come to fruition, and that knowledge of the area's history would be shared with residents and visitors alike.

Another of Arthur's achievements is one that cannot be found in any museum display or historical site. As a young man he had left school almost illiterate, but later in life his determination to research the history of the *Invincible* persuaded him to pursue self-study and become more proficient in reading and writing. Arthur expanded on his personal development to include public speaking, and in recent times he has given talks on pre-history in Langstone Harbour to students at local schools in the Portsmouth area. In 2016 he presented to members of The Society for Nautical Research (South) at the opening of the *Command of the Oceans* exhibition in The Historic Dockyard Chatham, regarding a collection of *Invincible* artefacts on display which were recovered and conserved by the original project team.

In 2014 Arthur sold his trusty companion, fishing boat *Wishbone*, which he had owned for more than 40 years – half his life. It was getting to be onerous maintaining the boat and inconvenient to attend to it in Langstone Harbour, as a dinghy was required to transfer between the boat's mooring and the shore. It must have pulled at his heartstrings to let go of the thing he had relied so much on to earn a living, but moreover the adventures and stories that boat had carried him through over the decades.

Though Arthur may have truly retired from fishing after letting go of *Wishbone*, he is still well known amongst local fishermen as the *'Old Man of the Sea'* — a nod to his lifelong maritime association and accomplishments. And by no means does Arthur sit around in his retirement wondering how to pass the time; he still occasionally walks the foreshore of Langstone Harbour searching for artefacts. In 2017 he found a Neolithic stone axe head in the mud.

Figure 44: The foreshore of Langstone Harbour at low tide

An exhibition devoted to the ship Arthur found – *Diving Deep: HMS Invincible 1744* – has been designed to showcase the artefacts recovered during the most recent excavation project at The Historic Dockyard Chatham and Portsmouth Historic Dockyard. Arthur and the team had agitated tirelessly for a dedicated museum gallery in Portsmouth to house the *Invincible* artefact collection, since the ship has always been associated with the Dockyard from the time she was towed into harbour as a war prize from the Battle of Cape Finisterre in 1747. However, the discovery of *Invincible* was eclipsed by worldwide attention for the wreck of King Henry VIII's flagship the *Mary Rose*, raised in 1982, which received major funding and support, leaving little in the way of opportunity for the *Invincible* Project. The National Museum of the Royal Navy has now pledged to house the newest collection of *Invincible* artefacts permanently within Portsmouth Dockyard, delivering satisfaction to Arthur that was a long time coming.

Arthur and Gina's family have carried on their time-honoured association with Portsmouth Dockyard and the Royal Navy. Their oldest son Kevin completed a Fitter and Turner apprenticeship and then took on a trade profession, dedicating thirty years of service to the Dockyard. Daughter Angela's husband Keith, who also hails from Pompey, served in the Royal Navy on several ships in the field of communications and is a veteran of the Falkland War.

Arthur and Gina are fortunate to have most of their family living in the Portsmouth area still today. Angela and Kevin, the two oldest children and their spouses Keith and Carole, live nearby. Youngest son Tony moved away to Portugal where he enjoys surfing and works in that industry. Grandsons Robin and Darryl are two successful men who both work in the field of computer engineering. Darryl and his wife Fran have a daughter and son themselves, giving Arthur and Gina the pride and joy of two great grandchildren. Great Granddaughter Lizzie, age eight, is following in Arthur's footsteps with a keen interest in flint knapping after he gave her a Bronze Age flint scraper that he found in Langstone Harbour. She loves to go on walks with him on Langstone's foreshore, hoping to be the next one who finds an artefact from ancient times past. Arthur says, '*she has it in her blood*' and believes one day she may even pursue archaeology herself. And Ethan, at age 3, loves to sit on Great Granddad's lap and look at the pictures in Arthur's archaeology and history books.

Figure 45: Daughter Angela & husband Keith

Figure 46: Son Kevin & wife Carole

Figure 47: Son Tony

Figure 48: Grandsons Darryl & Robin (right)

Figure 49: Fran with Great Grandchildren Ethan & Lizzie

Figure 50: Storytime

If you ever visit Portsmouth, take a stroll down the promenade of The Hard and there, close to Victory Gate, you will find a bronze statue of a young girl holding a coin and a man looking on.

Figure 51: The mudlarks' commemoration near Victory Gate

In 2008 Portsmouth City Council commissioned a commemoration of the mudlarks' history, and the statue and accompanying dedication plaques with names including Arthur's were unveiled on

26th March 2010. That spot overlooks the very place Arthur and other mudlarks worked and played so many years ago.

What is next for Arthur? He maintains an involvement in academic pursuits and is currently assisting John Bingeman as a researcher, investigating the historical significance of navy and military uniform buttons recovered from the wrecks of Royal Navy vessels *Pomone* (1811) and *Invincible* (1758). Arthur has built up a personal library of books concerning the military heritage of Britain, which he actively studies. Arthur still has contributions to knowledge ahead of him as he pursues his lifelong passion for history.

In January 2021 Arthur and Gina celebrate their 65th Wedding Anniversary – a significant milestone in their lives that few couples are lucky to achieve. Arthur says *'Marrying Gina is the finest thing I have ever done. She has supported me in all my endeavours.'*

Figure 52: Gina & Arthur in recent times

Credit – Illustrations

Cover: Design – John Broomhead.

Cover background image: Photographic reproduction - modified. Photograph – Daria Fomina. Image title – '*Ripples on blue sea water with white foam, natural sea background*'. Image ID – 1149424381. Used under Licence issued by iStock/Getty Images.

Front Cover inset: Photograph – John Broomhead. Image title – '*Arthur with Wealdon Stone Face*'. Reproduced by kind permission of Portsmouth Museum Service, Portsmouth City Council.

Back Cover inset: Photographic reproduction of print [partial] – John Broomhead. Artwork – R. Short. Publisher – J. Boydell, 1750. Image title – '…*Exact Stern-Views of His Majesty's Ships Invincible, Ruby and Isis…*'. Public domain work of art.

Figure 1: *The Common–Hard, Portsmouth* by G. Reinagle, 1834. Photographic reproduction. Photograph – G. Reinagle. Publisher – J. Dickinson, 1834. Image title – '*The Common–Hard, Portsmouth.*'. From Wikimedia Commons. Public domain work of art.

Figure 2: Mudlarks in Portsmouth Harbour, circa 1930s. Photographic reproduction. Photograph – unattributed. Image title – N/A. Image ID – IMG1358. © Portsmouth Publishing & Printing Ltd. Used under Licence issued by Portsmouth Publishing & Printing Ltd.

Figure 3: Bomb-damaged houses in Hambrook Street, Southsea. Photographic reproduction. Photograph – unattributed. Image title – N/A. Image ID – 1059 HAMBROOK STREET AREA W. © Portsmouth Publishing & Printing Ltd. Used under Licence issued by Portsmouth Publishing & Printing Ltd.

Figure 4: Gina & Arthur on her 21st birthday and engagement day. Photograph – Thomas Shepherd.

Figure 5: Gina & Arthur on their wedding day. Photograph – Marshall Photographers, Waterlooville.

Figure 6: *Daikoku* statuette found by Arthur. Photograph – John Broomhead.

Figure 7: Arthur fishing in Langstone Harbour in the early 1970s. Photograph – Melvin Gofton.

Figure 8: A sea bass catch aboard *Vanessa*, circa 1978. Photograph – Melvin Gofton.

Figure 9: Arthur's fishing boat, aptly named *Wishbone*. Photograph – Arthur Mack.

Figure 10: Leather cartridge case found on the *Invincible* wreck. Photographic reproduction – John Broomhead.

Figure 11: Jaime Broomhead and an *Invincible* rigging block, 1980. Photograph – John Broomhead.

Figure 12: Arthur & John Bingeman examining wreck artefacts. Photograph – Jane Bingeman.

Figure 13: John Broomhead's dive log entry from 13th June 1981. Photographic reproduction & original work – John Broomhead.

Figure 14: John Broomhead & Arthur (right) excavating the wreck. Photograph – © Graham Parker – www.rusalkaswim.com.

Figure 15: *His Majesty's Ship Invincible* by R. Short, 1751. Photographic reproduction of colourised print – Brent Piniuta. Artwork – R. Short. Publisher – J. Boydell, 1751. Image title – '...*Exact View of His Majesty's Ship Invincible, of 74 Guns...*'. Public domain work of art.

Figure 16: *Invincible stranded on Sunday 19th February 1758* by John R. Terry. Photographic reproduction – John M. Bingeman. Artwork – © John R. Terry. By kind permission of Joy Terry.

Figure 17: Arthur with *Invincible* artefacts aboard *HMS Victory* – early 1980s. Photograph – John M. Bingeman. By kind permission of the National Museum of the Royal Navy.

Figure 18: Robin Gibb opening the *Invincible* Exhibition. Photograph – © Ainsley Adams. By kind permission of Dwina Gibb and Keir Hailstone.

Figure 19: Robin Gibb & Arthur with an *Invincible* artefact. Photograph – © Ainsley Adams. By kind permission of Dwina Gibb and Keir Hailstone.

Figure 20: The dock where *Invincible* was built. Photograph – Arthur Mack.

Figure 21: 1ˢᵗ *Invincible* wreck buoy, the project team's dive boat *Ceres*, and the 6ᵗʰ *Invincible* beyond, 1984. Photograph – © Graham Parker – www.rusalkaswim.com.

Figure 22: Arthur & John Bingeman in *Wishbone*. Photograph – © Brian Lavery.

Figure 23: Arthur alongside the *Hazardous* (1706) wreck buoy. Photograph – John M. Bingeman.

Figure 24: Selsey Bill (top), Hayling Island and Portsea Island. Photographic reproduction. Photograph – © John Armagh. Image title – '*Photograph of Selsey Bill, Hayling Island and Portsea Island from the air*'. From Wikimedia Commons. Published under license: Creative Commons CC0 1.0 Universal Public Domain Dedication (https://creativecommons.org/publicdomain/zero/1.0/deed.en).

Figure 25: Arthur with survey equipment on Long Island. Photograph – unattributed.

Figure 26: Arthur & Michael J. Allen celebrating the publication of *Our Changing Coast*. Photograph – unattributed. Image title – N/A. Image ID – 912554. © Portsmouth Publishing & Printing Ltd. Previously published in the *Portsmouth News*. Used under Licence issued by Portsmouth Publishing & Printing Ltd. By kind permission of Michael J. Allen.

Figure 27: Arthur at the Sinah Circle site (outlined), Langstone Harbour. Photograph – John M. Bingeman.

Figure 28: John Bingeman's survey notes – Sinah Circle Structure. Original work – John M. Bingeman. Previously published by Hampshire & Wight Trust for Maritime Archaeology.

Figure 29: The Saxon log boat in-situ. Photograph – John M. Bingeman.

Figure 30: Saxon log boat on display in Portsmouth Museum. Photograph – John Broomhead. Reproduced by kind permission of Portsmouth Museum Service, Portsmouth City Council.

Figure 31: Arthur examining a burial urn in-situ. Photograph – John M. Bingeman.

Figure 32: Wealdon Stone Face. Photograph – John Broomhead.

Figure 33: Arthur's snake ring found in Portsmouth Harbour. Photograph – John Broomhead.

Figure 34: The medallion found by Arthur. Photograph – Anthony (Tony) Mack.

Figure 35: St Christopher ring from the mud of The Hard. Photograph – Anthony (Tony) Mack.

Figure 36: Arrival of the *Ordzhonikidze* in Portsmouth Harbour. Photographic reproduction. Image title – '*The Russian Sverdlov Class cruisers Ordzhonikidze arriving at Portsmouth Harbour this morning. April 1956 P009525*'. Alamy Photo Image ID: B55KF0. Trinity Mirror / Mirrorpix / Alamy Stock Photo. Used under Licence issued by Alamy Limited.

Figure 37: Lieutenant Lionel 'Buster' Crabb, RNVR. Photographic reproduction. Photograph – Coote, R G (Lt), Royal Navy official photographer. Image title – '*Lieutenant Lionel 'Buster' Crabbe, in diving apparatus at Gibraltar, April 1944.*' Image ID – A 23270. © Imperial War Museums. Used under Licence issued on behalf of the Trustees of Imperial War Museum.

Figure 38: Arthur at the stern of *Nicole* and Melvin Gofton at the helm. Photograph – Brent Piniuta.

Figure 39: Looking back at *Nicole* before descending on the wreck. Photograph – Brent Piniuta.

Figure 40: Arriving at the seabed. Photograph – Brent Piniuta.

Figure 41: John Broomhead examining *Invincible's* timbers. Photograph – Brent Piniuta.

Figure 42: John Bingeman & Arthur with an *Invincible* artefact. Photograph – Brent Piniuta.

Figure 43: The 'Original 3' – John Bingeman, Arthur & John Broomhead. Photograph – Brent Piniuta.

Figure 44: The foreshore of Langstone Harbour at low tide. Photographic reproduction. Photograph – © Editor5807. Image title – '*Langstone Harbour seen from Southsea, Hampshire during low tide.*' From Wikimedia Commons. Published under license: Creative Commons Attribution 3.0 Unported (https://creativecommons.org/licenses/by/3.0/deed.en) license.

Figure 45: Daughter Angela & husband Keith. Photograph – the Mack family.

Figure 46: Son Kevin & wife Carole. Photograph – the Mack family.

Figure 47: Son Tony. Photograph – the Mack family.

Figure 48: Grandsons Darryl & Robin (right). Photograph – the Mack family.

Figure 49: Fran with Great Grandchildren Ethan & Lizzie. Photograph – the Mack family.

Figure 50: Storytime. Photograph – the Mack family.

Figure 51: The mudlarks' commemoration near Victory Gate. Photographic reproduction. Photograph – Anthony Hatley. Image title – '*Bronze statue on The Hard at Portsmouth created by sculptor Michael Peacock in memory of 'the mudlarks' who staged mud fights.*' Alamy Photo Image ID: E8HHNK. Anthony Hatley/Alamy Stock Photo. Used under Licence issued by Alamy Limited.

Figure 52: Gina & Arthur in recent times. Photograph – the Mack family.

Notes

1. Spratt, H. P. *Isambard Kingdom Brunel.* Nature Publishing Group, 1958.

2. Lambert, Tim. A Brief History of Portsea, Portsmouth. *Portsea in the 18th Century.* http://www.localhistories.org/portsea.html (accessed 14 5, 2020).

3. Snippets from a Portsmouth Past. *The Common Hard.* https://snippetsfromaportsmouthpast.blogspot.com (accessed 11 4, 2019).

4. The Blitz in Portsmouth. *Air Raids During the Portsmouth Blitz.* https://welcometoportsmouth.co.uk/the%20blitz.html (accessed 11 13 2019).

5. Hind, Bob (*The News* – Portsmouth). *Huge blast at Gosport naval depot blew the roof off Fareham mansion: RETRO.* https://www.portsmouth.co.uk/retro/huge-blast-gosport-naval-depot-blew-roof-fareham-mansion-retro-1308493 (accessed 11 23, 2019).

6. Mack, Arthur T. *The Influence of the French on British Shipbuilding in the Eighteenth Century.* London: The World Ship Trust, 1992.

7. Fenwick, Valerie & Gale, Alison. *Historic Shipwrecks – Discovered, Protected & Investigated.* Stroud, Gloucestershire: Tempus Publishing, 1998.

8. Tweed, Ronald. *A History of Langstone Harbour and its environs in the County of Hampshire.* Dido Publications, 2000.

9,10. Allen, Michael J. & Gardner, Julie. *Our Changing Coast – a survey of the intertidal archaeology of Langstone Harbour, Hampshire.* Walmgate, York: Council for British Archaeology, 2000.

11,14. Satchell, Julie. *Long Island Project 2002, Langstone Harbour, Hampshire – Project Report.* Southampton, Hampshire: Hampshire & Wight Trust for Maritime Archaeology, 2003.

12,13. BBC News – Hampshire & Isle of Wight. *Museum home for Langstone Harbour Saxon logboat.* https://www.bbc.com/news/uk-england-hampshire-11409053 (accessed 12 15, 2019).

15. BBC News – Hampshire & Isle of Wight. *Ancient boat found buried in mud.* http://news.bbc.co.uk/2/hi/uk_news/england/hampshire/dorset/3082328.stm (accessed 12 18, 2019).

16. The Sally Port Hotel. *An all-time great spy / mystery story.* http://www.thesallyport.co.uk/the-sally-port-opens-its-doors.php (accessed 12 29, 2019).

17. The Dark Histories Podcast. *The Crabb Affair.* https://www.darkhistories.com/the-crabb-affair/ (accessed 12 30, 2019).

18,20. Imperial War Museum. *Non-Contact, Parachute Ground (Land) Mine Type GC.* https://www.iwm.org.uk/collections/item/object/30020471 (accessed 01 08, 2020).

19. Portsmouth Museum Service. *Portsmouth Reborn – Destruction and Reconstruction 1939-1974.* http://portsmouthmuseums.co.uk/collections/collection-a-portsmouth-reborn.html (accessed 01 08, 2020).

21. Bannister, Sam (*The News – Portsmouth*). *New board will tell the story of first dockyard.* Print edition – September 27th, 2014.

Bibliography

Lavery, Brian. *The Royal Navy's First Invincible 1744 - 1758 – The ship, the wreck, and the recovery.* Invincible Conservations (1744-1758) Limited, 1988.

Gardiner, Robert. *The Heavy Frigate: Eighteen-Pounder Frigates Volume 1, 1778-1800.* Conway Maritime Press, 1994.

Bingeman, John M. *The First HMS Invincible (1747-58) - Her Excavations (1980-1991).* Bingeman Publications, 2015.

Mack, A. T. *The Influence of the French on British Shipbuilding in the Eighteenth Century.* London: The World Ship Trust, October 1992 (1): 14-26.

Bingeman, John M. and Mack, Arthur T. *The dating of military buttons: second interim report based on artefacts recovered from the 18th-century wreck Invincible, between 1979 and 1990.* The International Journal of Nautical Archaeology, 1997 (26.1): 39-50.

Bingeman, John M., Bethell, John P., Goodwin, Peter, Mack, Arthur T. *Copper and other Sheathing in the Royal Navy.* The International Journal of Nautical Archaeology, 2000 (29.2): 218-229.

Printed in Great Britain
by Amazon